THURSDAY PEA SOUP

SPICED RYE BREAD

SCANDINAVIAN FEASTS

BEATRICE OJAKANGAS

PHOTOGRAPHY BY MICHAEL GRIMALDI

STEWART, TABORI & CHANG ▪ NEW YORK

To my dedicated partner and loving husband,
Richard Wayne Ojakangas
—B.A.O.

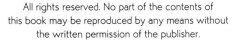

Text copyright © 1992 Beatrice Ojakangas
Photographs copyright © 1992 Michael Grimaldi

Prop stylist: Barbara Winfield
Food stylist: Sarah Greenberg
Photo Assistant: Marian Marseu

The publisher gratefully acknowledges the assistance of
Royal Copenhagen and Georg Jensen.

Published in 1992 by
Stewart, Tabori & Chang, Inc.
575 Broadway, New York, New York 10012

Library of Congress Cataloging-in-Publication Data

Ojakangas. Beatrice A.
Scandinavian feasts / Beatrice Ojakangas; photography by Michael Grimaldi.
p.   cm.
Includes index.
ISBN 1-55670-179-9
1. Cookery. Scandinavian. I. Grimaldi, Michael. II. Title.
TX722.A1044   1992
641.5948—dc20   91-37322
CIP

Distributed in the U.S. by Workman Publishing,
708 Broadway, New York, New York 10003
Distributed in Canada by Canadian Manda Group,
P.O. Box 920 Station U, Toronto, Ontario M8Z 5P9
Distributed in all other territories by
Little, Brown and Company, International Division,
34 Beacon Street, Boston, Massachusetts 02108

Printed in Japan.
10 9 8 7 6 5 4 3 2 1

Page 1: Swedish Berry Parfait, page 5: Swedish Onion Pie, Brie Pie,
page 7: Blueberry Cheesecake.

CONTENTS

Situated as Scandinavia is, in the northern part of the northern hemisphere, it really has only two seasons: summer and winter. Light, not temperature, has everything to do with the change in season.

Summer comes with Easter in the minds of Scandinavians, whether the ground is still covered with snow crystals or not. By the end of April, the days are as long as midsummer days in Minnesota. Beginning then, the long Scandinavian summer days are full of color, and people make the most of the extra hours of daylight and energy by enjoying the outdoors as much as possible. The foods of summer are themselves cause for celebration: tiny garden vegetables, lettuces, berries, and fruits; fresh fish, sometimes plump with roe, from the streams, lakes, and seas; and dairy products, rich and creamy. Breakfasts may be served early in the morning and suppers, at midnight. Coffee and sandwiches fit anywhere in between. All are frequently served outdoors, so family and friends can enjoy the lingering hours of light.

Winter, or at least the mood of winter, begins about the time that the school year starts in August or September. Mushrooms and game from the forests, simmered stews, and home-baked breads begin to sound very tempting. As the sun makes its way back to the southern hemisphere, the days become short, welcoming cozy, indoor meals. By December, lunch by candlelight fulfills the wintry desire for warmth and color.

Among all Scandinavians, once you break the ice, there is an abundance of hospitality. Breaking the ice usually begins with an invitation to coffee, which most Scandinavians drink by the gallon, often accompanied by wonderful cookies, cakes, and pastries. Alcoholic drinks are very expensive in Scandinavia and, depending on the occasion, either are served with abandon or not at all. Scandinavians, too, have discovered French wines, which while still expensive, are frequently offered. Finns make both white and red wines, as well as sparkling wines from red currants, all of which are very good. For native spirits, Danes, Norwegians, and Swedes lean heavily toward aquavit, a potato liquor flavored differently in every province of each country. But the Finns rarely serve aquavit, favoring instead their own clear spirit, vodka.

While researching this book, I was curious to find out whether there was anything *new* in the Scandinavian food world. The answer: yes and no. Scandinavians still know and appreciate their old favorite national dishes, which are served in school lunchrooms, highway truck stops, and are listed on the noon menu of almost every restaurant. The midday meal is still the preferred hot meal of the day. I was told I could have Thursday Pea Soup and Pancakes in any little café in Sweden and Finland, so long as it was Thursday. Throughout Denmark, "The Recipe"—taken from a post-World War II guide to good eating—is served in countryside restaurants as a noontime buffet. On the street in Oslo, Norway, I enjoyed the ever-popular *lompe,* a hot dog rolled in potato *lefse.* What did I drink with it? Coke.

Some of what *is* new comes from changes in the economy of Scandinavia. What was a rural economy has diversified. Today, women and men are frequently both at work out of the home, which means that meal patterns have changed and what people cook has changed (although the number of convenience foods is still minimal when compared with, say, the United States). Because of a greater international awareness of what is healthy, Scandinavians are eating less fat and more fresh foods, which means in winter more imported fresh vegetables and fruits. Imported foods are more expensive, which in turn prompts both mom and dad to go to work.

International food fashion has affected the offerings of Scandinavian restaurants, too. Outstanding chefs, such as Arne Brimi of Lom, Norway, who cooks only with organic ingredients; Erwin Lauterbach, chef of the Restaurant Saison in Copenhagen, and advocate of fresh and natural ingredients; and Gunnar Forsell of Stockholm's new Kållhagen, all advocate a new, lighter Scandinavian cuisine.

This book contains thirty-four menus, and I could have included many more, all featuring favorite Scandinavian foods. All of the recipes have been tested using ingredients available in the United States. None of the menus is engraved in stone, and many have dishes that are interchangeable, from one menu to another. But each menu captures something of the essence of Scandinavian cooking, whether old or new.

Danish

Finnish

Norwegian

Swedish

Whenever possible, I have included the Danish, Finnish, Norwegian, and Swedish names (in that order) for each recipe. They appear in the bars at the bottom of the recipe pages. Some recipes have the name from just one country, and that is because the dish may be known just in that one country.

If your favorite Scandinavian recipe or menu is not included, I am truly sorry. Many of my favorites are not included either, but one has to draw the line somewhere. You may find new favorites instead, and I hope you do. ❋

ACKNOWLEDGMENTS

My parents, in good Finnish tradition, taught me never to accept anything without offering to pay for it, especially if it was something I really needed. This book has left me deeply indebted to so many people for whom a simple "thank you" just doesn't seem to be enough.

First, there are my friends, family, and husband, Richard, who never limited their enthusiasm for *Scandinavian Feasts*. The encouragement and unending support of Elise Goodman, my literary agent has been invaluable. To Ann Campbell, my patient editor, Michael Grimaldi, our talented photographer, and food stylist Sarah Greenberg go special thanks. I'm grateful, too, for the enthusiasm of the staff at Stewart, Tabori & Chang. Thanks to Lise Lunge-Larsen, Bev Gronlund, Mary Boman, and Ann Campbell's mother for lending their personal Scandinavian treasures to be photographed. My thanks also go to Wendy Burrell for information on Scandinavian cheeses.

In order to write this book, I needed to take a fresh look at Scandinavian cooking today. Assisted by a couple of frequent-flyer tickets, and an extensive car-travel plan, my husband and I set off on an incredible tour. I would like to thank Pernilla Ullburger of the Swedish Tourist Board and Gunnar Rasmussen, both of whom enthusiastically pointed us toward a delightful variety of Swedish countryside inns: We stayed in an old farmhouse-style inn, a castle, a ski resort, an historic inn, a newly built inn, and a monastery. I wish to thank Carl Sandberg of Klockargården, Jan Anders Olsson and Jan Thelin of Åregården, Christian Giertta of Tanum's GestgIfverl, Peter Malmgren of Rusthållargården, Johan Milton of Munkklostret, and the staff of the beautiful new Kållhagen in Stockholm, for their hospitality, their enthusiasm for *Scandinavian Feasts*, and for sharing the secrets of regional Swedish foods. I learned so much from all of them.

It is hardly enough to thank Lillian Hess of the Danish Tourist Office in New York, who spent uncounted hours making contacts with bakeries, chefs, food specialists, tourist offices, and country inns throughout Denmark. A humble thanks goes to Bo Biilmann of Copenhagen, Kaj Handberg of Åalborg, and to the staff at the Viborg Tourist office. We laughed our way through Denmark as we were exposed to Danish *hygge*. Certainly, Danes are the jolliest people!

Thanks go to Per Brask at the Brygger Bauers Grotto in Viborg, Hans and Else Anderson at the Kongensbro Kro, Carl Petz at the Hvidsten Kro, Elisabeth Rudkobing in Aarhus, Ib Nielsen at the Sortebro Kro in Odense, Per Meyn and Bo Nielsen at Den Gamle Kro in Odense, Marianne Stagetorn at the La Glace Konditori in Copenhagen, Jorgen Jensen at the Kransekagehuset in Copenhagen, Ida "the queen of smørrebrød" Davidson, and Erwin Lauterbach, chef and owner of Restaurant Saison and the leader in the movement toward a new, lighter Danish cuisine.

My heartfelt thanks go to Ingrid Espelid Hovid, Norway's most outstanding food writer, and Arne Brimi, Norway's acclaimed young chef, for generously sharing their food knowledge, and to Embjorg Skamskar, a delightful lady, for taking me into her home to teach me how to make flatbread.

For years of enthusiastic support, I owe thanks to the staffs at Vaasan Mylly, the outstanding flour mill of Finland, Valio, Finland's foremost producer of dairy products, and Arabia, the producer of beautiful cookware and tableware. I am also indebted to Tellervo Anttila, Kaija Aarikka, Inga Aaltonen, Eva Salonen, and Anna Maija Tanttu, fellow home economists of Finland who have generously shared their expertise and recipes.

Tuhat kiitokset, Tusan Takk!

FRESH BERRIES WITH VANILLA CREAM SAUCE

BREAKFASTS

BAKED OAT PORRIDGE

FINNISH FARMHOUSE BREAKFAST

The old-fashioned Finnish farmhouse, a simple structure painted a deep barn-board red with crisp white trim, is mostly *tupa* on the main floor. The *tupa* is a combination kitchen-dining-living room that might also serve as sleeping quarters on smaller farms. Central to the room, and usually to the whole house, is a wood-fired masonry stove that has a brick oven built into it. The stove is always heated, except during the hottest days of summer, and throughout the nights the oven maintains a steady, low heat. ■ A baked porridge called *puuro,* which can be made of whole, cracked, or rolled oats, rye, barley, or wheat, or any combination of these grains, is daily fare in many Finnish farmhouses. I love it with a topping of toasted rolled oats, a sprinkling of cinnamon sugar, and cold milk. Some people prefer to sweeten their porridge with a spoonful of lingonberry preserves. Others add an "eye" of butter. Along with porridge, Finns usually serve bread, butter, and cheese. ■ In the springtime, the rhubarb stalks are plump and juicy, and the wild strawberries are ripe. Although when I make strawberry-rhubarb juice, I prefer to use a *mehu-maija,* the Finnish three-tiered steam-process juicer, one isn't necessary for the recipe given in this menu.

MENU

STEAMED STRAWBERRY-RHUBARB JUICE

GRAHAM RUSKS AND HARDTACK

SCANDINAVIAN CRISPBREADS
AND CHEESES

BAKED OAT OR RYE PORRIDGE

LINGONBERRY OR
CRANBERRY PRESERVES

STEAMED STRAWBERRY-RHUBARB JUICE

2 pounds rhubarb, cut into 1-inch cubes

2 pints fresh strawberries, halved

5 quarts water

1 cup sugar

As fruits and berries come into season, Finnish cooks gather and preserve them in the form of steamed juices. In the springtime, the first batch can be made from tiny, juicy wild strawberries and the early shoots of plump rhubarb stalks. Later, in the summer, juice can be made from raspberries, red currants, chokecherries, grapes from the vine, crabapples, cranberries, and, in the fall, from a whole variety of apples.

Simply sweetened to taste and served at room temperature or chilled, these juices are healthful and delicious. Mixed with an equal amount of ginger ale or lemon soda, they make great punches.

In a large, nonaluminum pot, combine the rhubarb, strawberries, and water. Bring to a boil over moderate heat, stirring occasionally. Continue to boil, stirring occasionally, for 15 minutes. Stir in the sugar and cook for one minute. Remove from the heat, cover, and allow to cool. When cooled, strain the juice. Serve at room temperature or chilled.

Approximately 2 quarts

Mansikkaraparperimehu

These rusks are made by splitting soft graham buns into two parts, then baking them again until they are crisp. They are delicious spread with butter and honey or marmalade. Finns and Swedes fill big jars with rusks and take them to their summer cabins where they eat them in place of bread.

In a large mixing bowl, dissolve the yeast in the warm water. Add the butter to the hot milk and set aside until the butter is melted and the mixture is cooled to lukewarm. Add the cooled butter mixture, salt, and sugar to the yeast mixture. Stir in the graham (or whole wheat) flour. Blend in enough of the bread (or all-purpose) flour to make a stiff dough.

Turn the dough out onto a lightly floured board and knead it until smooth and satiny, adding the remaining flour as necessary. Divide into four parts. Cut each part into eight pieces. Shape the pieces into smooth balls and place them on a lightly greased baking sheet. Cover and let rise until doubled.

Preheat oven to 450°F. Bake for 10 to 12 minutes or until browned. Remove the buns from the oven and cool them on a rack. With a fork, split the buns horizontally into two parts. Place on a baking sheet and place the baking sheet in a 400°F oven for 12 minutes or just until browned. Turn the oven off, and allow the rusks to dry there for 12 hours or overnight.

64 rusks

GRAHAM RUSKS

2 packages active dry yeast

½ cup warm water (105°F to 115°F)

½ cup (1 stick) butter, cut into tablespoons

1½ cups hot milk

1 teaspoon salt

1 tablespoon sugar

3 cups graham or whole wheat flour

3 to 3½ cups bread or all-purpose flour

Grahammikorppu

Grahamsskorpor

HARDTACK

¾ cup (1½ sticks) butter, melted

1½ cups buttermilk

3 cups flour

3 cups finely-ground rolled oats

1 teaspoon baking soda

1 teaspoon salt

Hardtack—also called crispbread—is a staple throughout Scandinavia, and there are many excellent varieties both homemade and store-bought. This one is a quick oatmeal crispbread. Grind the rolled oats for this recipe in a food processor fitted with a steel blade or in a blender.

Preheat oven to 375°F. Lightly grease four 11-by-17-inch cookie sheets.

In a large bowl, stir together the melted butter and the buttermilk. Add the remaining ingredients to make a stiff, sticky dough. Let it stand for 10 minutes (the dough will become less sticky). Divide into four parts and place one part on each cookie sheet. Using either a regular rolling pin, or one made especially for hardtack, roll the dough out to the edges of the cookie sheets (it will be very thin). Trim the edges and score the dough into 2-by-4-inch pieces. If you are using a plain rolling pin, pierce the dough all over with a fork. If you are using a hobnailed hardtack rolling pin, you do not need to pierce the dough. Bake for 20 to 25 minutes, until golden and crisp.

Approximately 112 crackers

Knaekkebrod

Näkkileipä

Flatbrød

Nackebrod

Cooked grains in their simplest form have always been the mainstay of rural Scandinavian cuisine. While perfect for breakfast, they are also often served for dessert with a fruit sauce poured over each serving. And leftover porridge can be pressed into a dish and chilled, then sliced, fried in butter, and served with strawberry jam and butter. This steaming porridge, baked all night in a slow oven, is wonderful on a chilly spring morning.

Combine the water, oats (or rye), and salt in a 2½-quart baking dish. Cover tightly. Place the dish in a pan filled with enough hot tap water to reach halfway up the sides of the dish and place in the oven. Set the oven at 250°F. Bake overnight, or for about 8 hours.

Serve hot with lingonberry or cranberry preserves or cinnamon and sugar, butter, and cream or milk.

8 servings

6 cups water

2 cups old-fashioned rolled oats, steel-cut oats, or cracked rye berries (available in health food stores)

¼ to ½ teaspoon salt

Lingonberry or cranberry preserves or cinnamon and sugar

Butter

Cream or milk

Kaurapuuro

Havregrøt

POTATO PANCAKES

SWEDISH COUNTRY BREAKFAST

As a guest in Sweden, whether in a friend's home or country inn, breakfast is an event to remember. Not only is there fruit juice and fresh fruit or berries (especially in the summertime), but fruit soup too. Jams and jellies, and a variety of both freshly baked breads and crisp-breads accompany platters of cheese and cured meats, tomatoes, lettuce, and cucumbers. There are always boiled eggs, kept warm in a cozy, and usually there is a hot dish such as this farmer's omelette, flavored according to what the garden is bearing, or these potato pancakes. Then there always is a cooked porridge or two with a selection of cream, milk, buttermilk, yogurt, and clabbered milk for topping, and, of course, a variety of pickled herring and smoked fishes, and wonderful homemade sausage. It goes without saying, that lots of good, fresh, strong coffee is imperative! ▪ Such an extensive menu seems a little ambitious, so I pared this one down to the basics. In fact, I often serve either the Swedish Farmer's Omelette *or* the Potato Pancakes. In the autumn, when the apples are best, I might add an apple cake to the menu.

MENU

SCANDINAVIAN FRUIT SOUP

SWEDISH FARMER'S OMELETTE

FRESH PORK SAUSAGE
(SEE PAGE 41)

POTATO PANCAKES WITH BACON,
SOUR CREAM, AND LINGONBERRIES
OR LINGONBERRY JAM

◎◎◎◎

SCANDINAVIAN FRUIT SOUP

¾ cup dried apricots or peaches

¾ cup dried pitted prunes

2 tablespoons golden raisins

2 tablespoons dark raisins

1 tablespoon currants

1 (3-inch) cinnamon stick

1 teaspoon grated orange peel

3 tablespoons quick-cooking tapioca

4 cups apple juice, cranberry juice, or water

¼ cup sugar

1 tart red apple, peeled, cored, and cut into 1-inch chunks

Heavy (whipping) cream

In the United States, we think of fruit soup as a dessert, but in Scandinavia it is offered on winter breakfast buffets, along with thick cream, which is poured over each serving.

Cut the apricots (or peaches) and prunes into quarters and place in a 2½-quart saucepan. Add the golden and dark raisins, currants, cinnamon stick, orange peel, and tapioca. Add the juice or water and let stand for one hour. Stir in the sugar. Place over moderate heat and heat to boiling, then reduce the heat and simmer, stirring occasionally, for 30 minutes, or until the fruit is tender and the soup is thickened. Add the apple, and cook for 10 minutes, or until the apple is tender. Remove from heat and cool. Pour the soup into a serving bowl, cover, and chill. Serve with cream.

6 servings

Frugtsuppe

Hedelmäkeitto

Fruktsuppe

Fruktsoppa

FRUIT SOUP

FARMER'S OMELETTE

FRESH PORK SAUSAGE

SWEDISH FARMER'S OMELETTE

¼ cup (½ stick) butter

1 medium-sized sweet onion, sliced

4 medium-sized potatoes, peeled and diced

1 cup finely diced ham

2 tablespoons fresh chives, minced

1 teaspoon dried dill weed

6 eggs

½ cup milk

1 teaspoon salt

½ teaspoon pepper

1 cup shredded mild farmer's cheese (such as *Bondost*) or Jack cheese

1 tomato, peeled and sliced

1 green pepper, seeded and sliced

1 cup sour cream (optional)

The winter version of this omelette may include only onions and potatoes. In the summertime, Swedes add garden vegetables as they come into season.

In a 10-inch nonstick, broilerproof omelette pan, melt the butter over medium heat. Add the onion and potatoes. Sauté for 15 to 20 minutes, until the potatoes are tender. Add the ham, chives, and dill.

Beat together the eggs, milk, salt, and pepper and pour over the sauté. Cover and cook over low heat for 15 to 20 minutes, until set. Sprinkle with half the cheese.

Preheat the broiler. Top the omelette with the tomato, green pepper, and remaining cheese. Broil until the cheese melts. Serve with sour cream.

6 servings

Bondomelett

POTATO PANCAKES

There are dozens of variations of the potato pancake throughout Scandinavia. At the Gøta Hotel on the banks of the Gøta Canal in central Sweden, they make theirs with coarsely shredded potatoes held together in a thin pancake batter consisting of eggs, milk, and flour. They are delicious served with crisp bacon, sour cream, and lingonberries or strawberry jam.

Rinse the potatoes in cold water and drain well. Place in a large bowl and mix in the flour, chives, milk, egg, salt, and pepper. In a heavy, preferably nonstick, skillet, over medium heat, cook the bacon until crisp. Remove the bacon slices from the skillet and drain. Hold the bacon slices on a plate lined with paper towel until ready to use. Spoon out all but 2 teaspoons of the bacon fat from the skillet.

Place the skillet over medium heat and spoon about ¼ cup of the potato mixture into the pan and flatten slightly to make a pancake. Cook until golden and crisp, about 3 or 4 minutes, on each side. Repeat this procedure with the remaining batter. Keep cooked pancakes warm until ready to serve.

Serve with the crisp bacon on top and lingonberries or whole, cooked or canned, cranberries on the side.

6 servings

8 medium-sized baking potatoes, pared and coarsely shredded

½ cup flour

2 tablespoons chopped chives

1 cup milk

1 egg

1 teaspoon salt

½ teaspoon freshly ground pepper

½ pound thick sliced bacon

Lingonberries or cranberries

Perunamunkit

Raggmunk

CLASSIC SCANDINAVIAN BREAKFAST

Tucked away in the rolling countryside of Sweden are homey, old-fashioned inns that serve the traditional cuisine of the area. Klockargården, in Tallberg, on the shores of Lake Siljan, is one such country inn. The guest rooms are charming, with comfortable beds, cozy feather comforters, scrubbed wooden floors, and colorful pots of geraniums on the window sills. ▪ Breakfast is served buffet-style. Typically, there is a selection of cheeses, herring, cold meats, crispbreads, and freshly baked breads and buns. There are also fresh seasonal fruits and stewed fruits served with cream or vanilla cream sauce. Eggs, boiled for five or ten minutes, are kept warm in a napkin-lined basket. In Norway, at the Roisheim Inn at Lom, they serve hot-from-the-oven baked cheese omelettes. ▪ In Denmark, at the Kongensbro Kro at Ans By, they serve rye butter buns, made of a yeasty, flaky pastry. Because of their rectangular shape, they are called *birkes* (bricks). ▪ The recipes included in this menu are a combination of my favorites from Sweden, Denmark, and Norway. Add to the menu your favorite fresh fruits, breads, and coffeecakes. The baked cheese omelette is terrific because it can be assembled ahead of time—as early as the night before—and baked at the last minute.

MENU

FRESH BERRIES WITH **VANILLA CREAM SAUCE**

DANISH RYE BUTTER BUNS

ORANGE AND BOYSENBERRY MARMALADES

NORWEGIAN BAKED CHEESE OMELETTE

VANILLA CREAM SAUCE

Cold and creamy, this slightly sweet sauce is perfect poured over all kinds of fresh fruits and berries. It also makes a marvelous sauce for a variety of hot apple desserts. Even the leaner version of this sauce—made with skim milk instead of cream—tastes smooth and rich.

In a heavy saucepan, beat together the egg, sugar, cornstarch, and cream (or milk). Stirring constantly, slowly bring to a simmer over low heat, and simmer 2 to 3 minutes, until slightly thickened. Remove from heat and cool, covered. When cooled to room temperature, stir in the vanilla. Cover again and chill. Before serving, fold in the whipped cream, if desired.

6 to 8 generous servings

1 egg

2 tablespoons sugar

2 tablespoons cornstarch or potato starch

3 cups light cream or milk (whole or skim)

2 teaspoons vanilla extract

1 cup heavy (whipping) cream, whipped (optional)

Vanillecremesovs

Vaniljakastike

Vaniljesaus

Vaniljsas

DANISH RYE BUTTER BUNS

2 packages active dry yeast (do not
   use quick-rise yeast)

½ cup warm water (105°F to 115°F)

1 cup warm milk (105°F to 115°F)

2 tablespoons sugar

1 teaspoon salt

2 eggs

½ cup (1 stick) butter, melted

2 cups light or dark rye flour

4 cups all-purpose flour

1½ cups (3 sticks) cold butter,
   preferably unsalted

½ cup (1 stick) butter, softened

GLAZE

1 egg, beaten

Coarse salt

Caraway seeds

Birkes

I enjoyed these brick-shaped flaky rye buns at the Kongensbro Kro, one of Denmark's outstanding country inns. Somewhat like Danish pastry, the yeast dough is rolled with butter into many thin layers.

In a medium-sized mixing bowl, dissolve the yeast in the water. Add the milk, sugar, and salt and let stand for 5 minutes, until the yeast foams. Beat in the eggs, melted butter, and 1 cup of the rye flour.

Measure the remaining rye and all-purpose flour into a large bowl. Slice the cold butter and add to the flour. Cut the butter into the flour until the pieces of dough are about the size of peas. Pour the yeast mixture over the flour mixture. With a rubber spatula, carefully fold the mixtures together just until the flour is moistened.

Cover the bowl and refrigerate for at least 4 hours and up to 2 days.

When ready to shape the dough, turn it out onto a lightly floured board. Knead gently to expel any air bubbles. Divide the dough into four parts. Shape one part at a time and leave remaining dough, covered, in the refrigerator.

Roll the dough out to make a large 16-inch circle. With a butter knife, spread the surface of the circle with 1 tablespoon of the soft butter. Fold the circle into thirds by overlapping the two sides across the center to form a rectangular strip. Roll out the strip to about 24 inches and then fold the strip into thirds by overlapping the ends across the center. Roll out the folded dough again to make a square about 16 inches across. Spread the surface of the square with 1 tablespoon of the soft butter and roll the dough up tightly, jelly-roll fashion. Flatten the roll slightly by pressing it down with the palms of your hands. Cut the roll into eight pieces of equal size. Place the pieces upright on a lightly greased baking sheet (with the seam-side down and the cut edges facing the sides of the baking sheet).

Repeat with remaining dough. Let rise in a warm place until doubled in size, about 2 hours.

Preheat oven to 400°F. Brush the buns with the beaten egg, then sprinkle lightly with the coarse salt and caraway seeds. Bake for 13 to 15 minutes, until golden and crispy. Remove the buns from the oven and cool on racks. Serve warm or cooled.

32 rolls

NORWEGIAN BAKED CHEESE OMELETTE

Cheese is the backbone of the Scandinavian breakfast, and this omelette is made with nutty Norwegian Jarlsberg. It is so quick, I sometimes make it for a late-night supper, too.

Preheat oven to 400°F.
Whisk together the eggs, water, and salt.
In a heavy, ovenproof casserole or frying pan, melt the butter. Add the onions, ham, and bell pepper and sauté over medium heat for 3 to 4 minutes, until the onions are bright green and the pepper is hot. Pour the egg mixture over the sauté and sprinkle with the cheese cubes. Bake for 15 to 20 minutes, until the egg mixture is set and the cheese is melted. Garnish with chopped parsley.

4 servings

4 eggs

¼ cup water

½ teaspoon salt

2 tablespoons butter

4 whole green onions, sliced

1 cup diced cooked ham

**1 red bell pepper, seeded, and sliced
into thin rings**

**12 ounces regular or lowfat Jarlsberg
cheese, cut into ½-inch cubes**

Chopped parsley, for garnish

Ostpanne

OVEN PANCAKE

BRUNCHES

Summer in Scandinavia is refreshing and energizing. It is the season when Scandinavians sit back, relax, and enjoy the beauty of nature and the fruits of the garden and forest. The days are incredibly long, and the nights are without real darkness, which helps the vegetables and fruits to ripen quickly. Everything seems ready at the same time and Scandinavian cooks take advantage of it. ■ Platters of steamed garden-fresh vegetables, like the one in this menu, are commonly served with thinly sliced, dry-cured reindeer, lamb, mutton, beef, or game. Arne Brimi, one of Norway's outstanding young chefs, led me on a tour of his impressive store of hanging home-cured meats: lamb and mutton, reindeer, and even bear. The method he and others commonly use to cure meat is a rustic, ancient procedure involving a dry cure using salt, similar to the method used in Italy to make prosciutto. If you are unable to obtain authentic cured meats, you can substitute thinly shaved smoked beef, ham, corned beef, or pastrami. In place of the chives in the scrambled eggs, you can substitute any other fresh herbs you have in your garden, such as chervil, thyme, tarragon, or basil.

MENU

POPPY SEED BUNS

SMOKED MEAT AND STEAMED
VEGETABLE PLATTER WITH
JARLSBERG CHEESE SAUCE

SCRAMBLED EGGS WITH CHIVES

RASPBERRIES OR STRAWBERRIES WITH
WHIPPED OR SOUR CREAM

POPPY SEED BUNS

Bread with poppy seeds is served only on very special occasions in Norway. Make these buns and keep the extras on hand in the freezer for special occasions.

I n a large bowl, dissolve the yeast in the warm water. Let stand for 5 minutes, until the yeast begins to foam. Stir in the milk, butter, and salt. Beat in 2 cups of the flour until smooth. Stir in additional flour, one cup at a time, until the dough is stiff. Cover the bowl and let stand for 15 minutes.

Turn the dough out onto a lightly floured board. Knead for 10 minutes or until smooth and satiny. Lightly grease the mixing bowl and return the dough to it, turning the dough over to grease the top. Cover and let rise in a warm place until doubled, about 1 to 2 hours.

Punch the dough down and turn it out onto a lightly oiled surface. Divide it into four parts. Divide each part into four more parts to make sixteen portions of dough. Shape each portion into a round bun and place it on a lightly greased baking sheet. Cover and let rise until doubled, about 45 minutes.

Preheat oven to 375°F. Brush the tops of the buns with the beaten egg white and sprinkle with the poppy seeds. Bake for 15 minutes or until buns are golden. Remove from the oven and transfer to cooling racks.

16 buns

2 packages active dry yeast

½ cup warm water (105°F to 115°F)

2 cups skimmed milk, scalded and cooled to 105°F to 115°F

2 tablespoons butter, melted

1½ teaspoons salt

5 to 6 cups bread or all-purpose flour

1 beaten egg white

2 tablespoons poppy seeds

Frobrød

SMOKED MEAT AND STEAMED VEGETABLE PLATTER WITH JARLSBERG CHEESE SAUCE

This dish is beautiful and colorful when you use all the fresh vegetables from your garden, steamed just until they are bright and arranged on a great big platter. Norwegians use a lot of very thinly sliced, salted, smoked reindeer or mutton, but sandwich meats make a good substitute. You'll need a large pot for steaming the vegetables.

1 whole cauliflower or small summer cabbage, washed and trimmed

1 pound new potatoes, scrubbed

½ pound tiny carrots, scrubbed, or large carrots peeled, quartered lengthwise, and cut into 2½-inch pieces

½ pound snow peas or freshly shelled peas

Jarlsberg cheese sauce

½ pound thinly sliced or shaved smoked beef, smoked ham, corned beef, or pastrami

Melted butter

Chopped parsley

JARLSBERG CHEESE SAUCE

2 tablespoons butter

2 tablespoons flour

1 cup milk

½ cup shredded Jarlsberg or Swiss cheese

Salt and white pepper

Place the cauliflower (or cabbage), potatoes, and carrots in a vegetable steamer or on a rack suspended over a deep pot filled with about 2 inches of water. Heat the water to boiling, and steam the vegetables until they are crisper-tender, 25 to 35 minutes. Add the snow peas during the last 10 minutes of cooking. If you use shelled peas, cook them separately in a pot with just enough water to cover until they are just tender, about 10 minutes.

Meanwhile, to prepare the Jarlsberg sauce, in a 2-quart saucepan, melt the butter over medium heat. Add the flour and cook, stirring, until the butter-flour mixture is bubbling and foamy. (The flour must be cooked long enough to eliminate its raw taste.) Remove the pan from the heat and whisk in the milk. Return the pan to the heat and cook, stirring, until the sauce is smooth, thick, and boiling. Blend in the cheese and continue cooking and stirring until it is melted and smooth. Add salt and pepper to taste.

Place the cauliflower (or cabbage) on a large serving tray and spoon the cheese sauce over it, or save the sauce to be served on the side. Arrange the potatoes, carrots, snow peas, and meats around the cauliflower (or cabbage). Drizzle melted butter over all the vegetables except the cauliflower (or cabbage), and sprinkle parsley over the entire platter. Serve immediately.

6 servings

Saltkøtt med nye grønnsaker

SMOKED MEAT AND STEAMED VEGETABLE PLATTER

JARLSBERG CHEESE SAUCE

POPPY SEED BUNS

DANISH ADVENT AFTERNOON BRUNCH

If you were invited to visit a Danish home on a Sunday afternoon in December, you would probably be served freshly made *aebleskiver* and glogg. Such a casual, friendly, warm get-together might be billed as a "glogg party," and adults and children alike would make decorations for the Christmas tree—even though the tree itself does not appear in the Danish home until Christmas Eve. ▪ The word glogg is the general Scandinavian term for a hot, spicy punch served most often during the holiday season. Everybody seems to have a favorite recipe, varying widely in alcoholic strength. I give one nonalcoholic recipe here and several more— both alcoholic and nonalcoholic—in following menus. ▪ The traditional Danish pancakes, called *aebleskiver*, are baked in a special cast-iron pan with rounded depressions for each pancake. They are delicious served hot out of the pan, dusted with powdered sugar, but can also be kept warm in a slow oven until you are ready to whisk all of them to a candlelit table. It is traditional to nestle an almond into one *aebleskiver*, and to give the person who finds it a special gift.

MENU

SPICED TEA GLOGG

RED WINE GLOGG
(SEE PAGE 53)

DANISH PANCAKES WITH SUGAR
AND MARMALADE

◎◎◎◎

SPICED TEA GLOGG

3 quarts water

1 teaspoon whole cloves

1 (3-inch) cinnamon stick

1 piece fresh ginger, about 1-inch
square, peeled

5 bags of tea of any variety, or 2½
tablespoons loose tea tied in a
cheesecloth bag

3 cups orange juice

1 cup lemon juice

1 to 1½ cups sugar

1 whole lemon, thinly sliced

1 whole orange, thinly sliced

At glogg parties, children are served a nonalcoholic glogg as they make paper baskets that will be used to decorate the Christmas tree. The baskets will be filled with candy and hung on the tree, which traditionally does not appear in the Danish home until Christmas Eve.

In a large nonaluminum kettle, combine the water, cloves, cinnamon stick, and ginger, and heat to boiling. Add the tea. Cover the kettle, remove it from the heat, and let steep for 5 minutes. Then remove the tea bags or leaves.

In another pan, heat the orange juice, lemon juice, and sugar over medium heat, stirring until the sugar is dissolved. Pour the hot fruit juice mixture into the spiced tea. Add the lemon and orange slices. Keep hot until ready to serve, but do not boil.

25 servings, about six ounces each

Tegløgg

Teeglögi

Teglögg

DANISH PANCAKES

When making these pancakes, you must use a special pan called, in Danish, an *aebleskivepande,* which is available in Scandinavian gift shops. It has seven rounded depressions that yield spherical pancakes. Although the *aebleskiver* may be filled with applesauce or jam, they are also delicious unfilled, served hot out of the pan with a sprinkling of powdered sugar.

In a large bowl, blend the butter, egg yolks, milk, and sugar. In a medium bowl, combine the flour, baking powder, salt, and cardamom. Stir the dry ingredients into the egg yolk mixture. In a clean bowl, beat the egg whites until stiff but not dry. Fold the egg whites into the flour—egg yolk mixture. Heat the aebleskiver pan over medium-low heat until a drop of water sizzles when it is dropped into the pan. (If the heat is too high, the centers of the pancakes will be doughy.) Spoon ½ teaspoon butter into each cup and let it melt. Spoon 1 rounded tablespoon batter into each cup. Cook for about 1 minute on each side, turning each pancake over with a knitting needle or long wooden skewer. If you wish to fill the pancakes, place 1 teaspoon applesauce or jam onto the center of the pancake before turning. For a traditional Advent party, place one almond into one of the aebleskiver. Dust each aebleskiver with powdered sugar and serve hot.

20 pancakes

½ cup (1 stick) butter, melted

3 eggs, separated

1 cup milk

2 tablespoons sugar

1½ cups flour

2 teaspoons baking powder

½ teaspoon salt

½ teaspoon freshly ground cardamom (optional)

Butter

Applesauce or jam (optional)

Powdered sugar

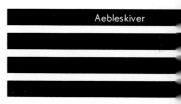

Aebleskiver

DANISH PANCAKES

PUFFY OVEN PANCAKE BRUNCH

It happens often that I bump into old friends and invite them over for a Sunday noon brunch. One of my favorite dishes around which I build the menu is this Finnish *pannukakku,* a showy baked pancake. The recipe is worth memorizing: Equal measures of eggs, milk, and flour are seasoned with a bit of salt and sugar and whisked or blended until smooth. The thin batter is baked in a pre-heated slope-sided pan (I have a favorite paella pan that works beautifully). I throw in a lump of butter that melts as the pan heats, then swish it around to coat the pan before adding the batter. As the pancake bakes, the edges rise and curl up the sides of the pan making a bowl-like shape, which I cut into wedges at the table. In the minutes that it takes for the pancake to cook, we enjoy a glass of sparkling juice, champagne, or apple cider, or in the winter, a cup of spiced orange or cranberry glogg. The pancake is delicious served with nothing but a squeeze of lemon juice and a sprinkle of powdered sugar, though I like to add whipped cream and a variety of fruits, such as sliced banana, fresh peach, nectarine, and pineapple chunks, or berries. To round out the meal, a salad of fresh cut-up fruit is a light complement and, for a bit of salt, some fresh pork sausage does the trick.

MENU

SPICED ORANGE GLOGG

CRANBERRY GLOGG

OVEN PANCAKE

LEMON WEDGES

WHIPPED CREAM

FRUIT SALAD

FRESH PORK SAUSAGE

@@@@

Orange juice combined with a fruity white wine (such as a Reisling or Rhine) or white grape juice and a hint of ginger and cardamom makes a delicious hot glogg.

In a nonaluminum saucepan or glogg pot, combine the orange juice, brown sugar, cardamom, and ginger. Heat slowly to a boil, stirring occasionally. Add the wine (or grape juice). Serve in warmed punch cups.

6 to 8 servings, 6 ounces each

SPICED ORANGE GLOGG

2 cups orange juice

¼ cup firmly packed brown sugar

1 teaspoon slightly crushed cardamom seeds

1 piece of fresh ginger, about 1-inch square, peeled, or ⅛ teaspoon ground dried ginger

1 (28-ounce) bottle white table wine, or four cups white grape juice

If desired, use cranberry liqueur in place of the cranberry juice, eliminate the sugar, and substitute red wine for white wine.

The night before you plan to serve this glogg, combine the wine (or grape juice), cranberry juice, cloves, ginger, and cinnamon sticks. Before serving, stir in the sugar to taste and heat to serving temperature, 150°F to 170°F, just below simmering. Ladle into small, warmed glogg cups or demitasse.

10 servings, 6 ounces each

CRANBERRY GLOGG

1 (28-ounce) bottle white table wine, or 4 cups white grape juice

4 cups cranberry juice

8 whole cloves

1 piece fresh ginger, about 1 inch, peeled

2 (3-inch) cinnamon sticks

¼ to ½ cup sugar

OVEN PANCAKE

8 eggs

2 cups milk

2 cups flour

2 teaspoons sugar

1½ teaspoons salt

½ cup (1 stick) butter

Lemon wedges

Powdered sugar

Fresh berries or other fruits

Whipped cream

This is a showy pancake that's great for brunch or supper. It is most spectacular just after baking, so have all the toppings ready in bowls to pass, and have the guests at the table waiting.

A 15-by-3-inch-deep paella pan is perfect for a single large pancake, but you can also divide the mixture among four 10-inch pie pans, with each pancake serving two.

In a large bowl, whisk together the eggs, milk, flour, sugar, and salt, until well blended. Let stand at room temperature for 30 minutes before baking (or mix ahead of time, cover, and refrigerate, but bring to room temperature before baking).

Preheat oven to 500°F. Put the butter into one 15-by-3-inch-deep paella pan, or divide it evenly among four 10-inch pie pans. Place in the preheating oven, just until the butter is melted. Remove from oven and swish the butter around so it coats the sides of each pan, and then pour the pancake batter into the pan or pans. Bake for 15 to 20 minutes or until the pancake has risen high up beyond the edges of the pan or pans, is golden on top, and has set in the center.

Transfer to the table immediately. Cut into wedges, squeeze lemon over each serving, and top with a sprinkling of powdered sugar, a spoonful of berries (or other fruit), and a dollop of whipped cream, if desired.

8 servings

Aeggekage

Pannukakku

Pannekake

Pannkaka

FRESH PORK SAUSAGE

Scandinavians are experts at making sausage. The practice goes back to when almost everybody lived on a farm and every family had its own "house pig." The pig was butchered in the fall so that the hams could be cured and smoked for Christmas dinner. The remainder of the meat was used for a variety of fresh cuts. The scraps and bits ended up in meat loaves, meatballs, pâtés, and sausages.

In this day and age, when most people buy their sausages, if you don't want to go through the trouble of pressing the meat into sausage casings, you can simply fry it up in patties. This sausage mixture has a smooth, almost creamy texture. Store uncooked links or patties in the freezer until you are ready to cook them.

Place the pork, salt, pepper, ginger, cloves, nutmeg, and potato flakes in the large bowl of an electric mixer or in a large food processor fitted with a steel blade, and mix until blended. Turn the mixer or processor onto high speed and slowly beat in the milk until the mixture is very light and pale pink in color.

Press the mixture into sausage casings (available from any butcher or meat market) and tie the ends with string, or shape the mixture into patties. Brown the sausages in a heavy skillet, turning occasionally, until cooked through, about 10 minutes.

Approximately 3 pounds of sausage

2½ pounds lean ground pork

2 teaspoons salt

¼ teaspoon pepper

¼ teaspoon ground ginger

¼ teaspoon ground cloves

Pinch of ground nutmeg

¼ cup instant potato flakes

2 cups milk

Sausage casings (optional)

Nøgle pølser

Makkara

Fleskepølse

Flöskkorv

SAINT LUCIA'S DAY CANDLELIGHT BRUNCH

Early on the morning of December 13th, Saint Lucia, the Queen of Light, enters the Swedish home, marking the beginning of the Christmas season. In some homes the youngest daughter descends the staircase wearing a crown of candles and offering traditional coffeebreads to the family. In one family that I know, all of the relations gather together at about six in the morning at the home of the grandparents to accept Saint Lucia buns from that year's appointed saint and to usher in the holiday season. ■ Many Swedish inns and hotels have a special Saint Lucia Day breakfast buffet, and most villages have a parade over which a young, blond girl

MENU

SEAFOOD OMELETTE

SLICED ORANGES WITH
CLOUDBERRY PRESERVES

SAINT LUCIA BUNS

ALMOND-STUFFED
BAKED APPLE HALVES

◎◎◎◎

reigns. In all of these celebrations, a golden, saffron-flavored sweet yeast bread is served. It may be shaped into buns, or a circular braid reminiscent of Saint Lucia's crown, or it may be shaped into traditional *Lussekatt,* or "Lucia Cats." Why the name? I really don't know, unless the two strips of dough, which are curled in opposite directions, are supposed to look like sleeping cats. There are, however, several more fanciful shapes and names for the saffron bread, including "Golden Chariots," "The Bishop's Wig," "The Apostles' Rings," "Christmas Wagons," and "Christmas Boars," all of which are made in many different provinces of Sweden.

SEAFOOD OMELETTE

One Swedish cook I know frequently serves this omelette as the hot course after a cold smorgasbord. It is as delicious at room temperature as it is hot, and if you reheat it as directed, it will puff up a second time.

Grease a 16-by-11-inch jelly-roll pan and line it with parchment paper. Butter the paper generously and sprinkle it with flour. Set aside. Preheat oven to 400°F.

Melt the butter in a saucepan. Add the flour and stir over medium heat for 1 minute. Add the milk, whisking briskly, and cook over low heat until the mixture is very thick and smooth. Remove from the heat and beat in all of the eggs at once, then the salt and nutmeg. Pour the mixture into the prepared pan and bake for 30 minutes, or until puffed and golden.

To prepare the filling, drain the juices from the lobster or crabmeat into a 2-cup or larger measuring cup. Add the heavy cream to equal 1⅓ cups. Melt the butter in a saucepan. Add the flour and cook over medium heat, stirring, for 2 minutes. Stir in the stock-and-cream mixture. Cook, stirring, until thickened and smooth. Season with the sherry, and salt and cayenne pepper to taste. Keep the filling warm.

Place a strip of waxed paper on a work surface and invert the baked omelette onto it. Remove the parchment paper from the bottom of the omelette. Spread the omelette with three-fourths of the filling. Using the waxed paper to lift the omelette, roll it up jelly-roll style, starting at a narrow end. Place the rolled omelette on a heatproof serving dish, seam-side face down. You may serve the omelette immediately or hold it, covered at room temperature, for up to one hour before serving. To reheat before serving, place the rolled omelette in a 400°F oven for 5 to 8 minutes. Before serving, top the omelette with the remaining filling. Garnish with crab claws (optional), dill, and lemon slices.

6 to 8 servings

½ cup (1 stick) unsalted butter

1 cup flour

2 cups milk

8 eggs, lightly beaten

½ teaspoon salt

¼ teaspoon nutmeg

8 ounces fresh or frozen crab claws, for garnish (optional)

Fresh dill, for garnish

Thinly sliced lemon, for garnish

FILLING

¾ pound freshly cooked lobster or crabmeat

1⅓ cups heavy (whipping) cream and seafood stock

2 tablespoons unsalted butter

2 tablespoons flour

2 tablespoons dry sherry

Salt and cayenne pepper

Hummeromelett

SAINT LUCIA WREATH AND BUNS

SAINT LUCIA WREATH AND BUNS

1 package active dry yeast

¼ cup warm water (105°F to 115°F)

¾ cup milk

½ cup (1 stick) butter

1 teaspoon saffron threads

½ cup sugar

¼ teaspoon salt

½ cup chopped raisins

2 eggs

3½ to 4 cups flour

1 beaten egg

In a large bowl, dissolve the yeast in the warm water. Scald the milk and add the butter to it; cool until the butter is melted and the mixture is lukewarm.

Preheat oven to 250°F. Lay the saffron threads on a piece of foil and place in the oven until toasted, about 5 minutes. Pulverize the toasted saffron with 1 teaspoon of the sugar, using a mortar and pestle or with the back of a spoon in a cup. Add 1 tablespoon of the milk-and-butter mixture.

Add the saffron mixture, milk-and-butter mixture, sugar, salt, raisins, and eggs to the yeast. Beat until blended. Stir in half the flour and beat until smooth and satiny. Add the remaining flour gradually to make a stiff dough. Let stand for 15 minutes.

Turn the dough out onto a lightly floured board. Knead for 10 minutes or until the dough is smooth and satiny. Place the dough in a clean, lightly oiled bowl. Turn the dough over to lightly oil the top. Cover and let rise in a warm place until doubled in size, about 1 hour.

Saint Lucia Braided Wreath

Punch the dough down and divide into three parts. Shape each part into a rope-like strand about 36 inches long. Braid the strands by aligning them vertically and alternately crossing each outer strand

Sahramileipä

Saffransbröd

over the center strand. Shape the braid into a circle and place on a greased or parchment-covered baking sheet. Pinch the ends together where they meet to seal the strands and to conceal the beginning and end of the braid. Brush with the beaten egg. Let rise for about 45 minutes or just until puffy. Preheat oven to 375°F. Bake for 20 to 25 minutes, until lightly browned, or until a wooden skewer inserted into the center of the dough comes out clean and dry. Cool on a rack.

1 large wreath

Saint Lucia Buns

Cover two baking sheets with parchment paper.

Punch the dough down and divide it into 32 parts. Shape each part into a rope about 8 inches long. Place two ropes side by side so they are parallel and touching each other. Curl all four ends toward the the center to form a square with rounded corners. Place the buns on the parchment-covered baking sheets. Let rise until puffy, about 30 minutes. Brush with beaten egg. Bake at 450°F for about 10 minutes, until golden. Cool on a rack.

18 buns

ALMOND-STUFFED BAKED APPLE HALVES

Preheat oven to 425°F. Core the apples and cut each one length-wise into two parts. Mix together the almonds, sugar, and water to make a paste. Fill the centers of the apples with almond paste, dividing the paste equally among them. Arrange them on a shallow baking pan, filled-side face up.

Drizzle the apples with the melted butter. In a small bowl, mix together the bread crumbs and brown sugar, and then sprinkle the mixture over the apples.

Bake the apples for 25 minutes or until tender. Serve with heavy cream or Vanilla Cream Sauce.

8 servings

4 large Granny Smith or other tart baking apples

½ cup blanched almonds, very finely chopped

¼ cup sugar

2 tablespoons water

1½ tablespoons butter, melted

½ cup fine dry bread crumbs

2 tablespoons brown sugar

Heavy (whipping) cream or Vanilla Cream Sauce (see page 23)

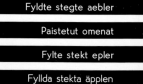

Fyldte stegte aebler

Paistetut omenat

Fylte stekt epler

Fyllda stekta äpplen

STRAWBERRIES AND CREAM CAKE

MARZIPAN KRINGLE

LUNCHES

Helvi Sipilä is a distinguished and dynamic Finnish woman with a long list of credits to her name, including several years of service in the United Nations. ■ One blustery December day, I was privileged to be invited into her home in Tapiola, a planned community in a suburb of Helsinki. The wind all but blew my husband and me through the door as we rang the bell, and Helvi greeted us with a tray of hot, strong glogg in demitasse—a welcome greeting as we were chilled to the bone. ■ The table was set with crisp white linens. The baked cheese came to us sizzling from the oven, and we spooned soufflé-like portions onto our plates. She accompanied the cheese with red beet salad, rye buns, and, for dessert, Finnish Plum Pudding, a thick cinnamon-and-rum-flavored fruit soup made with prunes. In the living room, afterward, we had ginger cookies and coffee. It was a most memorable lunch. ■ The buttermilk egg cheese can be made up to a week ahead of time, and though it is wonderful served fresh, when it is baked it is transformed into a cross between a crustless quiche and a cheese soufflé. Often I serve it as a hot dessert, sauced with raspberry, lingonberry, or cloudberry jam that I have thinned down with a bit of juice or fruit-flavored liqueur.

MENU

RED WINE GLOGG

RYE ROLLS

BAKED BUTTERMILK EGG CHEESE

RED BEET SALAD WITH SOUR
CREAM DRESSING

FINNISH PLUM PUDDING

SPICY GINGER COOKIES
(SEE PAGE 241)

◎◎◎◎

RED WINE GLOGG

Elisabeth Rudkoping is famous among her friends for the simplicity of her glogg recipe: Heat two 28-ounce bottles of red table wine with one 28-ounce bottle of red vermouth and a cup of sugar. Pour the heated mixture into cups holding a few raisins and blanched almonds and serve.

The following recipe is hardly more complex. For the best flavor, steep the spices in the sugar water for a few hours—or even a few days—and at the last minute, strain the mixture into the red wine, heat it just until hot, and serve. Remember that alcohol evaporates at 172°F: If you let the mixture boil the glogg will be mild indeed!

Several hours or days in advance, combine the water, sugar, cloves, cinnamon stick, and cardamom seeds in a saucepan. Bring to a boil, cover, and let stand until cold. Store in a covered jar or container until ready to use.

When you are ready to serve the glogg, pour the red wine into a nonaluminum saucepan or glogg pot. Strain the spice mixture into the wine. Heat to between 150°F and 170°F, just below simmering. Do not boil. Serve hot.

6 servings, about 6½ ounces each

1½ cups water

½ cup sugar

5 whole cloves

1 (3-inch) cinnamon stick

½ teaspoon cardamom seeds, slightly crushed

1 (28-ounce) bottle dry red wine

Julegløgg

Punaviiniglögi

Rodvin Glögg

BAKED BUTTERMILK EGG CHEESE

4 quarts whole milk

2 quarts buttermilk

4 eggs

1 teaspoon salt

1 teaspoon sugar

To make a significant amount of this cheese, you need to start with a lot of milk. (According to the cheesemaker's rule of thumb, it takes ten pounds of milk to produce one pound of cheese.) You will need your largest kettle—it may be a canning kettle—a big colander or strainer lined with several layers of cheesecloth, and a mold that will hold about 8 cups and has drain holes on the bottom. Finns have beautifully carved traditional wooden cheese molds, but you can also use a metal salad mold in which you have punched holes to drain the cheese overnight. This cheese will not keep for more than a week.

Pour the whole milk into a large kettle. Heat slowly to prevent burning, stirring often, until the milk comes to a boil. Meanwhile, in a medium-sized bowl, mix together the buttermilk and eggs. When the milk has come to a boil, stir in the buttermilk mixture very slowly and continue to cook just until the solids start to separate. Remove the kettle from the heat and stir in the salt and sugar. Cover and let stand until the curds rise to the surface, about 45 to 60 minutes.

Line a large colander or strainer with several layers of cheesecloth and set it over a large pot to catch the whey. Pour the cheese mixture into the cheesecloth-lined strainer. Allow to drain completely, about 1 hour.

Line a wooden (or metal) cheese mold with two layers of damp cheesecloth. Spoon the curds into the mold. Gather the cheesecloth over the top and place the mold in a larger pan—either hung from the rim or placed on a rack so that the mold does not rest on the bottom—to catch the drippings. Place a weight on top of the mold and refrigerate overnight.

Either unmold the cheese and serve chilled with fresh fruit, or preheat oven to 450°F, unmold the cheese onto a baking dish, and bake for 15 to 20 minutes, until the top is browned, and serve hot.

2 pounds

Munajuusto

Ostkaka

BAKED BUTTERMILK EGG CHEESE

RED BEET SALAD WITH SOUR CREAM DRESSING

RED BEET SALAD WITH SOUR CREAM DRESSING

1 cup finely chopped pickled herring (optional)

3 cups finely diced cold beets, freshly cooked or canned

1 medium-sized tart apple, peeled and diced

½ pound new potatoes, boiled, peeled, and diced

⅓ cup finely chopped dill pickle

⅓ cup finely chopped sweet onion

3 tablespoons white wine vinegar

¼ cup vegetable oil

1 teaspoon salt

½ teaspoon freshly ground black pepper

Chopped fresh parsley or dill, for garnish

DRESSING

1 cup heavy (whipping) cream, softly whipped, or sour cream

1 tablespoon fresh lemon juice

3 tablespoons beet juice

Salt and white pepper

If you choose to use herring in this salad, you might arrange all of the individual ingredients on a platter in a striped fashion, which will allow those who don't care for herring to avoid it. Blending all of the ingredients together will produce a red salad because the beets will color everything. In either case, the dressing—also colored by the beet juice—is most often served separately.

Mix together in a serving bowl or arrange on a platter the herring, beets, apple, potatoes, pickle, and onion. In a small bowl, mix together the vinegar, oil, salt, and pepper and drizzle over the salad. Sprinkle chopped parsley or dill around the edges. Cover and refrigerate until ready to serve.

To make the dressing, just before serving, combine the cream (or sour cream), lemon juice, and beet juice and season with salt and pepper. Serve in a bowl on the side.

6 servings

Sildsalat

Rossolli

Silsalat

Sillsalad

FINNISH PLUM PUDDING

Pudding made with prunes is a traditional Finnish Christmas dessert. This recipe calls for potato starch, which produces a beautifully clear, thickened juice, but arrowroot is a good second choice. You can find potato starch—sometimes called potato flour—in Scandinavian food specialty shops and in some gourmet or health food stores.

Combine the prunes and water in a heavy 2-quart saucepan. Add the cinnamon stick. Heat to boiling and cook until the prunes are very soft, 20 to 30 minutes. Transfer the prunes to a dessert bowl, reserving the prune liquid left in the saucepan. Remove and discard the cinnamon stick.

In a small bowl, stir together the cold water and the potato starch (or arrowroot) until smooth. Heat the prune liquid to boiling and slowly stir in the starch mixture. Simmer until thickened and transparent. Add the rum (optional). Pour the thickened liquid over the softened prunes and cover until cooled, to prevent a skin from forming on the top of the pudding. Serve chilled with whipped cream spooned on top of each serving.

6 servings

2 cups pitted prunes

3 cups water

1 (3-inch) cinnamon stick

½ cup cold water

2 tablespoons potato starch or arrowroot

1 tablespoon dark rum (optional)

Slightly sweetened whipped cream

Luumukiisseli

SWEDISH PANCAKES

THURSDAY PEA SOUP AND PANCAKES

Pea soup is a favorite throughout Scandinavia, where the combination of soup and pancakes is not an unusual one. In Sweden and western Finland, Thursday is the traditional day to eat this meal, and it is served all over: in small cafés, in the cafeterias of schools and places of work—and even in the army—as well as in most homes. When pea soup and pancakes are on the menu for a dinner party during the winter, the meal is usually preceded by a small cup of hot glogg or Swedish Punch, a sweet rum-flavored spirit. ■ Prob-

MENU

THURSDAY PEA SOUP

SPICED RYE BREAD

SWEDISH PANCAKES WITH SOUR CREAM AND LINGONBERRIES

◎◎◎◎

ably the most famous Thursday Pea Soup is the fatal bowlful served to the Swedish king Erik XIV, eldest son of beloved King Gustav Vasa, who succeeded his father in 1560. Erik, learned and accomplished but considered to be feeble-minded and violent, was imprisoned by his brothers. After many years of trying to escape, one Thursday he was given a serving of pea soup laced with arsenic, which ended his life. ■ In the town of Vadstena in Sweden, you can visit his prison cell in the castle and, if it is Thursday, have pea soup and pancakes in the café.

THURSDAY PEA SOUP

2 cups dried whole Swedish yellow
peas or yellow split peas

2 quarts water

1 (about 1½ pounds) smoked pork
shank or hock

1 medium onion, sliced

½ teaspoon thyme

½ teaspoon marjoram

Salt and pepper

If using Swedish yellow peas, rinse and pick over the peas, place them in a large pot, add the water, and let soak overnight. If you cannot find whole Swedish yellow peas, substitute yellow split peas, which do not need to be soaked, but can be cooked immediately.

Add the pork, onion, thyme, and marjoram. Bring to a boil, reduce the heat to a simmer and cook until both the pork and the peas are tender, 1½ to 2 hours. Add more water if necessary.

Remove and discard the bones from the pork. Cut the meat into cubes and return them to the soup. Season with salt and pepper.

6 to 8 servings

Hernekeitto

Artsoppa

SPICED RYE BREAD

This somewhat sweet bread is flavored with orange, anise, fennel, and caraway, which together give the bread its distinctive aroma.

In a medium-sized saucepan, heat the milk to scalding. Remove from the heat and add the water, butter (or shortening), molasses, sugar, orange rind, fennel, anise seed, caraway seed, and salt. Set aside until the mixture has cooled to approximately 110°F.

In a large mixing bowl, stir the yeast into the warm water. Let stand until the yeast begins to foam, about 5 minutes. Stir in the cooled milk mixture.

Stir in the rye flour and beat until the mixture is very smooth. Let stand for 15 minutes.

Stir in 2 cups of the bread (or all-purpose) flour and beat the dough until it is smooth. Cover and let stand for 1 hour.

Stir in enough of the remaining flour to make a stiff dough. Turn the dough out onto a floured board and knead until smooth and satiny, about 5 minutes.

Wash the bowl, lightly grease it, and then return the dough to it. Cover with plastic wrap and set in a warm place (85°F) to rise until doubled, about 1 hour.

Grease two 9½-by-5½-inch loaf pans or three 8-inch round cake pans.

Punch the dough down and turn it out onto a lightly oiled surface. Divide it into two or three equal parts. Shape each part into a loaf and place it in one of the pans, smooth-side up.

Let rise in a warm place until almost doubled, about 30 minutes. Preheat oven to 375°F. Bake the loaves for 35 to 40 minutes or until a wooden skewer inserted into the center comes out clean.

Remove the loaves from the oven and turn out of pans onto a cooling rack. Brush the tops of the loaves with butter (it will melt as it comes into contact with the hot surface of the bread).

Two 9½-by-5½-inch loaves, or three 8-inch round loaves

1 cup milk

1 cup water

3 tablespoons butter or shortening

½ cup light molasses

⅓ cup sugar

1 tablespoon freshly grated orange rind

1 tablespoon each crushed fennel, anise seed, and caraway seed

2 teaspoons salt

2 packages active dry yeast

¼ cup warm water (105°F to 115°F)

2 cups light or medium rye flour

4 to 5 cups bread or unbleached all-purpose flour

Butter, at room temperature

| Sigtebröd |
| Ruislimppu |
| Siktebrød |
| Limpa |

SWEDISH PANCAKES

½ cup flour

1 tablespoon sugar

¼ teaspoon salt

1 cup milk

½ cup heavy (whipping) cream

3 eggs

2 tablespoons butter, melted

Sour cream and lingonberry,
strawberry, or raspberry preserves

These pancakes are traditionally served with lingonberries or lingonberry preserves, as a dessert following Thursday Pea Soup. Swedish cooks use a special cast-iron pan called a *plattpanna,* which has seven shallow depressions, three inches in diameter. You can find these pans in Scandinavian gift shops and gourmet cookware stores. Otherwise, use an ordinary griddle and simply make small pancakes.

C ombine the flour, sugar, and salt in a mixing bowl. Stir in the milk, cream, eggs, and melted butter and blend until smooth. Brush the griddle with butter and place it over medium-high heat. To form each pancake, drop 1 tablespoon of batter onto the griddle. After 1 to 2 minutes, when the edges begin to brown, turn each pancake over with a narrow spatula, and cook the other side for 1 to 2 minutes, or until golden. Serve immediately with sour cream and preserves.

4 to 6 servings

| Lapper |
| Ohukkaat |
| Lapper |
| Plättar |

IRONS AND TOOLS FOR
PANCAKES, WAFFLES, CRISPBREADS,
AND COOKIES

BIRTHDAY PARTY LUNCHEON

irthdays—as well as name days—are important in Scandinavia, especially when the person being honored is either a child or has reached a magical age, such as fifty. In most homes, guests are seated at the table for the celebration, although if there is a big crowd, food might be served buffet-style. The variety of toppings and breads for make-your-own sandwiches might include cold meats and cheeses, but in this menu I have provided a recipe for a traditional shrimp and herring sampler. Each sandwich is built on a single slice of buttered bread and is eaten with a knife and fork. Sandwiches will vary according to each guest's tastes in much the same fashion as an individual salad from a salad bar would. ■ I love both of the birthday cakes in this menu. The marzipan-filled *kringle* is a pretzel-shaped Danish pastry, crusty with almonds. The Strawberries and Cream Cake is a simple sponge cake that is filled with fresh berries and whipped cream. Norwegians call this cake *bløtkake*, which translates as "wet cake," because they fill the sponge layers with berries and cream a few hours ahead so that the juices are absorbed and the cake is juicy and moist when it is served. Swedes often soak the layers in Swedish Punch, a sweet rum-flavored spirit.

MENU

SANDWICH PLATTER

SCANDINAVIAN CRISPBREADS

MARZIPAN BIRTHDAY KRINGLE

STRAWBERRIES AND CREAM CAKE

◎◎◎◎

SANDWICH PLATTER

It is typical of Scandinavians to present a variety of cold foods with which guests can build their own sandwiches. This recipe will serve eight to twelve people.

O n a large platter, arrange the lettuce leaves and pile the shrimp in one place. Drain the herrings and arrange on the platter along with the eggs, tomatoes, mushrooms, radishes, and green onions. Cover and chill until ready to serve.

To prepare the dressing, whip the cream until stiff peaks form. Blend in the lemon juice, salt, and white pepper. Add curry powder to taste.

Serve the dressing alongside the platter of sandwich fixings and assorted breads.

For 8 to 12 guests

2 heads Bibb or Boston lettuce, washed and separated

½ pound cooked shrimp, chilled

1 (8-ounce) jar marinated herring bits in sour cream

1 (8-ounce) jar marinated herring bits in wine sauce

6 hard-boiled eggs, peeled and halved

2 large tomatoes, thinly sliced

2 cups sliced mushrooms

1 cup sliced radishes

½ cup sliced green onion

Assorted dark and light breads, thinly sliced

DRESSING

1 cup heavy (whipping) cream

2 tablespoons lemon juice

½ teaspoon salt

¼ teaspoon ground white pepper

Curry powder

Smørrebrødplade

Voileipälautanen

Smørebrødsauser

Smörgåsarplatta

MARZIPAN BIRTHDAY KRINGLE

1 package active dry yeast

1 tablespoon sugar

½ cup warm milk (105°F to 115°F)

1 cup heavy (whipping) cream, at room
temperature

3½ cups flour

¼ cup sugar

1 teaspoon salt

1 teaspoon freshly ground cardamom

½ cup (1 stick) firm unsalted butter,
cut into tablespoons

ALMOND FILLING

1 (8-ounce) package almond paste,
about 1 cup

½ cup chopped, blanched almonds

½ cup sugar

1 teaspoon cinnamon

1 teaspoon almond extract

TOPPING

Approximately ½ cup sugar

1 egg white, beaten

¼ cup sliced almonds

Fødselsdagskringle

This irresistible birthday cake has a buttery, flaky yeast-risen pastry—which requires 12 hours of refrigeration—and an almond paste filling. It is twisted into a pretzel shape and coated with sliced almonds. Throughout Scandinavia, the symbol of the pretzel marks the bakery section of a supermarket or a bakery shop on the street.

I n a small bowl, combine the yeast, sugar, and milk. Let stand until the yeast dissolves and begins to foam, about 10 minutes. Gently stir in the cream.

In a large bowl, combine the flour, sugar, salt, and cardamom. Cut in the butter until the batter resembles coarse meal. Fold in the yeast mixture just until all of the dough is moistened. Cover and refrigerate for 12 to 24 hours.

To prepare the filling, just before rolling out the dough, blend together the almond paste, almonds, sugar, cinnamon, and almond extract.

Turn the chilled dough out onto a lightly floured surface. With a rolling pin, pound the dough until flattened to about a 2-inch thickness, then roll the dough out to make a 24-inch square.

Spread the filling to within 1 inch of the edges of the square and roll the dough up as tightly as possible.

Sprinkle the sugar for the topping on the work surface. Roll the dough firmly into the sugar to coat it well, and, at the same time, stretch it to form a log of dough measuring 36 to 40 inches long.

Cover a baking sheet with parchment paper. Place the roll on the paper in the shape of a pretzel. Brush the surface with the egg white and sprinkle with the almonds. Cover and let rise for 45 minutes, or until puffy but not doubled. Preheat oven to 375°F. Bake for 25 to 30 minutes, until golden.

Approximately 16 servings

STRAWBERRIES AND CREAM CAKE

The basic layers of this popular celebration cake are so simple that you can memorize the recipe: one cup each of eggs, sugar, and flour, plus one teaspoon each of baking powder and vanilla extract. Although this cake can be filled with anything you like, including all varieties of jams, my first choice is fresh strawberries.

Preheat oven to 350°F. Line the bottoms of two 9-inch round cake pans with parchment paper and coat the paper with non-stick cooking spray. In the large bowl of an electric mixer, beat the eggs until frothy. Raise the speed to high and add the sugar gradually, beating until very thick and lemon-colored, scraping the sides of the bowl often.

In a separate bowl, stir together the flour and baking powder. Reduce the speed of the electric mixer to low and slowly add the flour mixture to the whipped eggs. Mix just until blended. Blend in the vanilla.

Pour the batter into the two prepared cake pans, spreading it to the edges. Bake for 25 to 30 minutes, or until the center of the cake bounces back when touched. Remove the cake layers from the oven and cool.

To prepare the filling, whip the cream until stiff peaks form. Add the sugar and vanilla.

Remove the cakes from the pans. Invert one layer on a serving plate so that the flat side is face up.

Spread half the whipped cream on top and cover with a generous layer of sliced strawberries (or other fruit). Place the second layer on top of the fruit so that the flat side is face up. Top the cake with the remaining whipped cream and fruit.

Serve immediately or refrigerate up to 2 hours, then serve.

8 to 12 servings

1 cup (4 or 5 large) eggs, at room temperature

1 cup sugar

1 cup flour

1 teaspoon baking powder

1 teaspoon vanilla extract

FILLING

1 to 2 cups heavy (whipping) cream

2 tablespoons powdered sugar

1 teaspoon vanilla extract

1 quart fresh strawberries or other fresh fruits, sliced

Flødelagkage

Mansikkakakku

Bløtkake

Jurdgubbstårta

DILL-STUFFED WHOLE SALMON

PICNICS

In Norway, the weather isn't all that reliable, but Norwegians love to plan outdoor parties. When Lisa Lunge-Larsen's son was baptized, this celebration feast was served in Lisa's backyard. Actually, whether for a wedding, anniversary, birthday, or other special occasion, whenever Norwegians celebrate in the summertime, this is likely to be the menu. "There's always lots of dill, dill, dill!" Lisa explains. "It has to be the *new* dill, not the old stuff that already has seeds on it." ▪ Norwegians love desserts, and sometimes they will serve another selection, such as poached pears with chocolate sauce, in addition to the rum pudding. But the *kransekake,* the towering almond wreath cake made of graduated rings, is always the crowning treat, served with the coffee and cognac. ▪ *Kransekake* is also served on Christmas and on *Sytende Mai,* May 17th, Norway's independence day, when it is decorated with national flags and cracker bonbons. I was once invited to celebrate the 17th of May in the States with a dozen families of Norwegian descent. In keeping with contemporary Norwegian traditions, some wore national costumes and all wore red, white, and blue—the colors of the Norwegian flag. We sang the Norwegian national anthem and paraded down the street, alongside a convertible automobile playing Norwegian music. Children and adults alike waved Norwegian flags, and when the parading was done, we enjoyed our *Sytende Mai* feast.

MENU

DILL-STUFFED WHOLE SALMON

THREE SOUR CREAM SAUCES

NEW POTATOES WITH DILL

SWEET-SOUR CUCUMBER SALAD

TRADITIONAL ALMOND WREATH
CAKE OR BUTTER COOKIE ALMOND
WREATH CAKE

PEARS WITH CHOCOLATE SAUCE
AND WHIPPED CREAM

RUM PUDDING

COFFEE AND COGNAC

◎◎◎◎

If you are having a large party, you will need to cook one eight-pound salmon for every twelve guests. This can be done on the barbecue or in the oven. To assure the best flavor, be sure to use lots of young dill, not dill that has already gone to seed. Dried dill weed is an acceptable alternative if fresh dill is not available.

Preheat the barbecue (or oven to 400°F). Wash and dry the fish inside and out. Place it on a piece of heavy-duty aluminum foil that is large enough to generously wrap around the fish. Blend together the butter, garlic, salt, and pepper and smear it inside the fish. Stuff the fish with the whole young dill, or sprinkle the inside generously with the dried dill weed.

Wrap the fish tightly in the foil. Place it on the barbecue with coals banked on either side, so that the fish is not directly above the coals (or in the oven). Cover the barbecue with a lid and cook over slow coals until the fish flakes when tested with a fork, or until an instant reading thermometer inserted in the center of the flesh registers 120°F, about 25 to 30 minutes. If using a barbecue, turn the fish once, halfway through cooking.

When the fish is done, remove the foil and transfer the fish to a serving plate or plank. To serve, lift off the skin, then lift off portions of salmon, cutting through just to the backbone. When all the meat is removed from one side of the fish, lift off the backbone and serve the second fillet, cutting down to the skin.

12 servings per fish

1 (7- to 8-pound) whole Norwegian salmon, cleaned

½ cup (1 stick) butter

2 cloves garlic, chopped

1 teaspoon salt

½ teaspoon white pepper

1 large bunch young dill, or ¼ cup dried dill weed

Grillet laks med dill

THREE SOUR CREAM SAUCES

CUCUMBER SOUR CREAM SAUCE

1 (1-pound) European-style cucumber

2 teaspoons salt

1 cup sour cream

1 tablespoon lemon juice

1 tablespoon finely chopped green onion

Cucumber Sour Cream Sauce

When making this sauce, I prefer to use European-style cucumbers, sometimes called burpless, because they have fewer seeds and are more fleshy and flavorful than the waxed variety.

Peel the cucumber and split it in half lengthwise. Scrape out the seeds and finely chop the remainder. Sprinkle the chopped cucumber with the salt, and chill for at least 2 hours. Drain well. Mix with the sour cream, lemon juice, and green onion. Let stand for about 30 minutes before serving to allow the flavors to blend.

2 cups

APPLE SOUR CREAM SAUCE

2 medium-sized Granny Smith apples

1 cup sour cream

1 tablespoon lemon juice

Salt

Apple Sour Cream Sauce

This might seem a bit unusual, but the flavor of the tart apple is quite nice with the barbecued salmon.

Pare, core, and coarsely chop the apples. Stir together the apples, sour cream, and lemon juice. Season with salt. Let stand for 30 minutes to allow the flavors to blend.

2 cups

MUSTARD SOUR CREAM SAUCE

2 tablespoons sugar

2 tablespoons Dijon-style mustard

3 tablespoons wine vinegar

¾ cup sour cream

1 teaspoon lemon juice

1 teaspoon dried dill weed

Salt and pepper

Mustard Sour Cream Sauce

This sauce is good with almost any grilled or baked fish.

In a small bowl, whisk together the sugar, mustard, vinegar, and sour cream, until blended. Add the lemon juice and dill weed. Season with salt and pepper. Cover and refrigerate until ready to serve.

1 cup

SWEET-SOUR CUCUMBER SALAD

This all-Scandinavian favorite is easily prepared, but there are slight variations in each country. In Denmark, for instance, they don't like salads that are sour, so the lemon or vinegar may be cut by half. In Finland, quite often they add sour cream to the salad. In all cases, however, it is best made with new dill sprigs and the cucumbers must be sliced paper-thin!

Scrub the cucumber and slice paper-thin. Place the slices in a medium-sized bowl. Mix the lemon juice (or vinegar), sugar, salt, and pepper and pour over the cucumbers. Sprinkle with the chopped dill. Refrigerate for 3 hours to allow flavors to blend. Drain. Garnish with dill sprigs and serve.

12 servings

2 large European-style cucumbers

½ cup lemon juice or white wine vinegar

½ cup sugar

1 teaspoon salt

Dash white pepper

4 tablespoons chopped fresh new dill, or 4 teaspoons dried dill weed

Fresh dill sprigs, for garnish

Agurkesalat

Kurkkusalaatti

Agurkesalat

Inlagd gurka

TRADITIONAL ALMOND WREATH CAKE

1 pound (3 cups) almonds, blanched,
    unblanched, or a combination

1 pound (3 to 4 cups) powdered sugar

3 tablespoons flour

3 egg whites, slightly beaten

ROYAL ICING

1 pound (3 to 4 cups) powdered sugar

1 to 2 egg whites

1 teaspoon almond extract

Made of almond dough rings, this beautiful and festive cake stands like a tower, and is traditionally decorated with flowers, flags, and marzipan candies. The dough can be made with blanched or unblanched almonds, or with a mixture of the two. With unblanched almonds, the cake has a golden brown hue and is chewy. The easiest way to make a *kransekake* is to use the special ring molds that are sold in Scandinavian cookware catalogues or specialty shops. Or, you can use the original, trickier method of cutting the strands of dough into the different lengths and turning them into circles, all by hand.

To prepare the dough rings, pulverize the almonds in a blender or food processor. In a large bowl, blend together the almonds, powdered sugar, and flour. Mix in the egg whites to make a smooth and pliable dough. Knead the dough well, using the dough hook of an electric mixer, if desired. The dough will be firm but pliable enough to handle.

Preheat oven to 350°F.

To bake with ring molds: Grease the ring molds well and dust with flour. Cut off portions of the dough and shape into ropes the thickness of a finger, in lengths to fit the various sizes of the rings. Fit the ropes into the rings, smoothing the dough where the ends join. Place the filled rings on baking sheets. Bake for 10 minutes or until pale gold. Cool. Remove the rings from the molds and brush off any loose flour.

To bake without ring molds: Cover several cookie sheets with parchment paper. Cut off portions of the dough and shape into ropes about the thickness of your thumb (slightly thicker than described above), each one inch longer than the previous, beginning at 4 inches and ending at 18 inches. You will have 15 strands. Shape each strand into a circle and place on the parchment-covered baking sheets. Bake for 10 minutes or until pale gold. Cool.

Kransekage

Kransekake

Kransekaka

To make the Royal Icing, place the powdered sugar in the large bowl of an electric mixer. Add one egg white and the almond extract. Mix until smooth and well blended. If necessary, add part or all of the second egg white. The icing needs to be thin enough to press through the fine tip of a pastry bag. (In place of a pastry bag, you can use a cone made from waxed paper. Snip off the bottom of the cone to form a fine-tip opening.) Spoon the icing into a pastry bag (or a waxed paper cone).

To assemble the cake, place the largest cookie ring on a serving plate. Press the Royal Icing through the pastry bag (or waxed paper cone) in a zigzag pattern all the way around the ring. Top with the next largest ring. Repeat the zigzag piping procedure. Continue stacking and frosting the rings to form a balanced tower. Decorate the top with a fresh rose and the sides with flags, flowers, marzipan candies, or cracker bonbons, using the Royal Icing to adhere them to the cake.

To serve the cake, lift the top part of the tower off, and break the remaining rings into 2- or 3-inch pieces.

Approximately 48 servings

BUTTER COOKIE ALMOND WREATH CAKE

1 cup (2 sticks) unsalted butter, at
    room temperature

1 cup almond paste, at room
    temperature

1 cup powdered sugar

1 teaspoon almond extract

2 egg yolks

2½ cups all-purpose flour

Royal Icing (see page 74)

This butter cookie version of the traditional *kransekake* is a little easier to handle than the one made with pure almonds. In fact, it is no more difficult to mix up than a big batch of butter cookie dough. For this version, though, you must use the special baking rings described in the Traditional Almond Wreath Cake recipe (see page 74).

In a large mixing bowl, cream together the butter, almond paste, and sugar, until very smooth. Blend in the almond extract and egg yolks. In a separate bowl, stir together the salt and flour, then blend into the butter mixture. Chill the dough for 30 minutes.

Preheat oven to 350°F.

Follow traditional kransekake directions for baking in ring molds, assembling, and serving (see page 74).

Approximately 48 servings

Kransekage

Kransekake

Kransekaka

PEARS WITH CHOCOLATE SAUCE AND WHIPPED CREAM

6 ounces (6 squares) semisweet
  chocolate

½ cup heavy (whipping) cream

¼ cup sugar

2 tablespoons butter

1 tablespoon rum

12 freshly poached or canned large
  pear halves, chilled

Whipped cream

When fresh pears are in season, Norwegians poach them to make this classic dessert.

In a small bowl, over simmering water, combine the chocolate and cream, stirring until the chocolate is melted. Add the sugar and stir until it dissolves completely. Remove the bowl from the heat and add the butter and rum.

Before serving, arrange one pear half in each serving dish. Spoon the chocolate sauce over it and top with the whipped cream.

12 servings

Paere belle helene

RUM PUDDING

Not to be confused with *Rømmegrøt* (see page 199), a sour cream pudding served at Norwegian wedding celebrations, this recipe results in a light and fluffy rum pudding similar to a bavarian cream.

Soften the gelatin in the cold water. In a large metal bowl, beat the egg yolks, gradually adding the sugar. Beat until light and fluffy. Whisk in the cream (or milk), until blended.

Place the bowl holding the egg mixture over a pan of boiling water and cook, whisking, until smooth and slightly thickened. Remove from the heat and add the gelatin-water mixture, stirring until blended. Set the bowl over ice water or refrigerate, stirring occasionally, until thick and syrupy but not set, about 15 to 25 minutes. Add the rum flavoring.

Whip the egg whites until stiff. Fold the egg whites and whipped cream into the partially set pudding. Turn into a serving bowl and chill for 3 to 4 hours, or overnight, until set.

12 servings

2 envelopes unflavored gelatin

½ cup cold water

6 eggs, separated

½ cup sugar

2 cups light cream or milk

3 tablespoons rum, or ½ teaspoon rum extract

1 cup heavy (whipping) cream, whipped

Rombudding

Rummipuuro

Romgrøt

Romfromage

DALECARLIA PICNIC STEW AND WAFFLES

Dalecarlia is a colorful part of the province of Dalarna in the north-central part of Sweden. It is the land of red-and-white houses, hand-carved, painted wooden horses—a symbol of Sweden—waffle cottages, maypoles, picnic stews, and summer-long celebrations. ▪ The waffles that are served in waffle cottages are baked in irons that separate each one into five small hearts, which when attached are called a *lagg*. When broken into individual sections they are eaten like cookies, with jam and sweetened whipped cream or sour cream in the middle. Waffle cottages are open all winter to serve skiiers. In the summertime, when visitors come to enjoy the midnight sun, the waffle cottages also add an old-fashioned stew, called *söpåror*, to the menu. This special stew is often made in huge outdoor kettles over an open fire, and served at community picnics. While I usually think of stew as a wintertime food, it is actually quite a pleasant dish to serve al fresco in the summer. A classic thin bread made with dried, ground peas, and fresh cheese are traditional accompaniments to the stew. In this menu, I have suggested rye bread, which I am assured is perfectly acceptable.

MENU

MEAT AND VEGETABLE STEW

RYE BREAD

CRISP HEART-SHAPED WAFFLES

FRESH BERRIES

SWEETENED WHIPPED CREAM OR
SOUR CREAM

◉◉◉◉

CRISP HEART-SHAPED WAFFLES

MEAT AND VEGETABLE STEW

1 pound beef chuck or stew meat

1 pound lean, boneless pork shoulder

6 medium-sized potatoes (about 1½ pounds), pared

4 medium-sized carrots, pared

1 rutabaga (about 1 pound), pared

2 onions, sliced

1 tablespoon salt

¼ teaspoon white pepper

3 to 4 cups water

Chopped parsley

In Dalecarlia, this stew is frequently the main course for large community picnics. I have, however, reduced the quantities here to more manageable household amounts.

Cut the meats into 1-inch cubes. Cut the potatoes and carrots into slices about ½-inch thick. Quarter the rutabaga and cut into ½-inch slices.

Layer the meats and vegetables, including the onions, in a 4- or 5-quart heavy Dutch oven or casserole with a tight-fitting lid. Sprinkle with the salt and pepper. Pour in the water until it just covers the ingredients. Cover and place in the oven. Set oven at 350°F. Bake for 3 to 3½ hours, until all of the ingredients are very tender. Sprinkle with parsley and serve directly from the casserole.

8 to 10 servings

Söpåror

There are lots of different recipes for waffles—one for every Scandinavian cook, I suppose—but almost inevitably the waffles are heart-shaped. This one makes crisp, fragile waffles that can be served either hot or cold with sweetened whipped cream or sour cream, and berries or jam.

Preheat a waffle iron. In a medium-sized bowl, beat together the flour, water, ¼ cup of the cream, sugar, vanilla, baking powder, and salt, until smooth. In a separate bowl, whip the remaining cup of the cream, until stiff, and fold it into the batter.

Spoon the batter into the preheated waffle iron and bake until golden on both sides, about 4 minutes total. Transfer to a wire rack. Serve warm or cooled.

8 to 10 waffles

1¼ cups flour

¾ cup water

1¼ cup heavy (whipping) cream

2 tablespoons sugar

2 teaspoons vanilla extract

2¼ teaspoons baking powder

⅛ teaspoon salt

Flødevafler

Rapeat Vohvelit

Fløtevafler

Frasvåfflor

MIDSUMMER'S PICNIC

Midsummer's Day, June 24th, is celebrated in all of Scandinavia, but with quite different culinary customs. Swedes usually eat fish of some kind—pickled herring, salt-cured salmon *gravlax*, or even fresh poached fish—accompanied by boiled new potatoes with fresh-from-the-garden dill, and tiny, wild strawberries. Norwegians eat *rømmegrøt* (a cream pudding; see page 199) and sandwiches of thin crispbread and shaved cured reindeer, mutton, or lamb. The Finns might celebrate with boiled new potatoes with dill and lightly smoked salmon. ■ To decorate for the occasion, throughout Scandinavia, small birch trees are cut down and placed on either side of the entrance to the house and to the garden. Homes, cars, fences, and maypoles are also decorated with leafy branches and freshly cut flowers. The night of Midsummer's Eve is the time to tell tales of supernatural beings and magical powers, and the dew collected then is said to have healing properties. On Midsummer's Day, the maypole is raised in the center of the village square and everybody gathers around it. This is a day when many couples choose to speak their vows. For each marriage that takes place, a flag is added to the pole. Once the pole is raised, the dancing begins and it continues through the night. There is an old Finnish saying that if you sleep on Midsummer's Night, you will be sleepy all summer.

MENU

DILL-MARINATED SALMON FILLETS

THREE MUSTARD SAUCES

DANISH BLUE CHEESE SALAD

NEW POTATO SALAD

OVEN-FRIED CHICKEN

TOMATOES AND ONIONS

SCANDINAVIAN CRISPBREADS
AND BUTTER

STRAWBERRIES AND WHIPPED CREAM

SCANDINAVIAN OAT BARS

◎◎◎◎

DANISH BLUE CHEESE SALAD

DILL-MARINATED SALMON FILLETS

1 pound fresh salmon fillets, or fresh frozen boneless Norwegian salmon sides, with skin

¼ cup sugar

2 tablespoons coarse salt

1 tablespoon black peppercorns, coarsely crushed

4 tablespoons fresh dill, chopped, or dried dill weed

1 tablespoon aquavit or cognac

Gravadlaks

Graavi Lohi

Gravlaks

Gravlax

Salmon cured with dill, salt, and pepper is one of the great delicacies of Scandinavia—and one of the easiest dishes to prepare. The basic recipe is two parts salt to one part sugar, although some people prefer half and half. The fish does not require any other seasoning, but some cooks add white or black pepper, aromatic seed mixtures, dill, or other herbs.

Although Scandinavians would never do this, I recommend a quick-freeze if you are using fresh domestic fish. It will kill possible parasites and will make the fish easier to slice thinly. The freezing, which takes four to six hours, can be done after you pack the fish into the cure.

If the salmon is fresh, rinse, pat dry, and wrap the fillets separately in heavy-duty foil. Freeze for 48 hours. If using frozen salmon, proceed with the next step without thawing the fish.

Combine the sugar, salt, and peppercorns. Remove the fish from the freezer. Unwrap the fish and place the foil in a shallow glass dish. Lay the fish fillets, skin-side down, on top of the foil. Sprinkle with the dill, then the sugar mixture. Drizzle with the aquavit (or cognac). Leaving one fillet skin-side down, top it with the second fillet, skin-side up, sandwiching the seasonings in between. Close the foil securely using a drug-store wrap (align the long edges of the foil together above the fish and fold them down to make a lengthwise seam on top of the fish, then fold in the ends of the foil against the fish to form an airtight packet). Place a board and weights on top of the fish. Refrigerate for at least 48 hours, turning the packet several times, always replacing the board and weights on the packet. While the fish marinates, prepare and refrigerate one or more of three mustard sauces (see page 87).

To serve, remove the fish from the packet and scrape off the seasonings. With a very sharp knife, slice the fish on the diagonal and as thinly as possible, detaching each slice from the skin. Curl slices of the gravlax into cone shapes, and arrange on a platter or individual serving plates. For an attractive presentation, spoon the mustard sauces between the slices. Serve with thinly sliced rye bread.

12 appetizer servings

Gravlax is usually served with a mustard sauce, and these are three of my favorites. The sauces can be refrigerated in a tightly covered jar for several days.

Brown Sugar Mustard Sauce

Stir together the brown sugar and mustard, until well blended. Turn the mixture into a small bowl and sprinkle with the dill.

⅔ cup

Dark Mustard Sauce

In a deep bowl, mix together the prepared mustard, dry mustard, sugar, and vinegar to make a paste. Slowly whisk in the oil until it is the consistency of thick mayonnaise. Stir in the dill.

Approximately ⅔ cup

Dill Mustard Sauce

In a bowl or blender, combine the vinegar, mustard, egg yolk, sugar, salt, and dill weed. Slowly whisk or blend in the salad oil to make a smooth, thick sauce.

¾ cup

BROWN SUGAR MUSTARD SAUCE

⅓ cup firmly packed dark brown sugar

⅓ cup whole-grain mustard

Chopped fresh dill or dried dill weed

DARK MUSTARD SAUCE

¼ cup dark, highly-seasoned prepared mustard

1 teaspoon dry mustard

3 tablespoons sugar

2 tablespoons white vinegar

⅓ cup vegetable oil

3 tablespoons chopped fresh dill

DILL MUSTARD SAUCE

2 tablespoons white wine vinegar

2 tablespoons Dijon-style mustard

1 egg yolk

1 tablespoon sugar

¼ teaspoon salt

¼ teaspoon dried dill weed

7 tablespoons salad oil

DANISH BLUE CHEESE SALAD

1 quart small, new leaves of garden or butter lettuce

1 small bunch baby radishes, thinly sliced

2-inch length of cucumber, sliced paper-thin

1 sweet onion, thinly sliced

¼ pound crumbled Danish blue cheese

Pinch each of salt, pepper, dry mustard, and sugar

2 tablespoons wine vinegar

4 tablespoons salad oil

Made with the first tender lettuce of springtime, mild onion, and thinly sliced cucumber, this salad has a fresh taste. To slice the cucumbers paper-thin, use a Scandinavian cheese shaver.

Wash and dry the lettuce and turn it into a bowl. Add the radishes, cucumber, and onion. Sprinkle with the blue cheese.

In a small bowl, mix together the salt, pepper, mustard, sugar, and vinegar. Whisk in the salad oil. Just before serving, stir the dressing again and pour over the salad.

4 servings

Salat med Danablu

This potato salad is best when made with freshly dug potatoes from the garden. Little red potatoes from the market are a good second choice. No need to peel them.

Cook the potatoes in just enough water to cover them, until tender, 20 to 25 minutes. Cool and cut into ½-inch slices.

In a straight-sided glass bowl, layer the potatoes, sprinkling the layers with the onion and parsley, and top with the beets. Sprinkle with the chives. In a small bowl, blend together the vinegar, oil, salt, and pepper. Pour the dressing evenly over the potato mixture. Cover and chill for 1 to 2 hours.

4 servings

NEW POTATO SALAD

2 pounds tiny new potatoes

2 tablespoons chopped onion

2 tablespoons minced parsley

1 (16-ounce) can or jar pickled beets, diced and drained

2 tablespoons chopped chives

2 tablespoons wine vinegar

6 tablespoons salad oil

1 teaspoon salt

¼ teaspoon pepper

SCANDINAVIAN OAT BARS

These are so quick to make and so good to eat that you will want to keep them in your cookie jar year-round.

Preheat oven to 375°F. Lightly butter an 11-by-17-inch jelly-roll pan.

Melt the butter and let cool for 5 minutes. In a large bowl, stir together the oatmeal and melted butter. Stir in the sugar and egg whites until blended (the mixture will be somewhat crumbly). Press the oatmeal mixture into the prepared pan and smooth the top. Bake for 30 to 35 minutes, or until golden brown. Cut into squares while still warm but do not remove from the baking pan until cold.

80 2-inch squares

1 cup (2 sticks) butter

3½ cups quick-cooking oats

1 cup sugar

2 egg whites

FINNISH FIRESIDE STEAM-SMOKED FISH FEAST

For most of July and August, Finns take to their *mökki,* or cottages, to enjoy fresh food and lakeside relaxation. ▪ At my cousins' small cottage in the lake district of Finland, the pantry is well-stocked with jars of hardtack and whole grain rusks. There is a small garden for leaf lettuce, new potatoes, tomatoes, little carrots, peas, onions, and dill. The woods and lake are filled with berries and fish, respectively. ▪ Often, on the seemingly endless summer evenings, they steam-smoke trout. First, the fish is wrapped in a layer of waxed paper and a layer of wet newspaper. Then it is placed by the coals of the fire and cooked through by turning the package over as it is steamed and charred. The wrapping is then cut away and the skin is peeled back, so that everyone can lift tender portions onto their plates. When I'm not visiting my family in Finland, I repeat this procedure in my fireplace at home with very good results. Fish cooked in this manner has a lovely, mildly smoked flavor that needs no more adornment than a squeeze of lemon and a drizzle of melted butter.

MENU

FIRESIDE STEAM-SMOKED FISH

BOILED NEW POTATOES

OLD-FASHIONED CREAMY LETTUCE SALAD

CARAWAY RYE RUSKS

FRESH RASPBERRIES AND CREAM

◉◉◉◉

This is a great method for cooking almost any fresh game fish on a campfire, so long as you have paper with you, and the fish weighs at least 2 pounds. If you are concerned about the ink in the newspaper, use unprinted newspaper, unrecycled brown paper, or parchment paper.

1 (2- to 3-pound) whole trout, bass, or other game fish

Fresh dill, parsley, or other herbs

Salt and pepper

Melted butter

Clean the fish well and stuff it with the fresh sprigs of herbs. Sprinkle inside and out with salt and pepper. Wrap the fish in waxed paper, then in several layers of newspaper or brown paper so that the packet is about 6 inches thick through the middle. Dip the package into water to moisten the outer layer.

Place the package on the coals of a campfire, or a fire in a fireplace, and let the paper burn slowly around the fish.

When the wrap has burned down to the waxed paper, the fish is done. This takes about 20 to 25 minutes.

Peel off the paper and serve the fish hot. Serve with melted butter.

4 servings

Savustettu Kala

FIRESIDE STEAM-SMOKED FISH

OLD-FASHIONED CREAMY LETTUCE SALAD

1 quart fresh lettuce or wild edible
greens

½ cucumber, peeled, seeded, and cut
into thin strips

1 hard-boiled egg

1 teaspoon prepared mustard

½ teaspoon salt

½ teaspoon sugar

1 tablespoon lemon juice

½ cup heavy (whipping) cream,
whipped

Gathering wild edible greens is one of the activities that Finns enjoy at their summer cabins. Another is tending a garden patch to produce tender young greens, as well as herbs, for salads such as this one. The dressing recipe is an old-fashioned one.

Rinse the lettuce (or greens) leaves well, and wrap them in paper towels to dry. Place the wrapped leaves in plastic bags and chill to crispen.

Before serving, tear the leaves and place them in a salad bowl. Add the cucumber strips.

In a small bowl, mash the egg yolk with the mustard, salt, and sugar. Add the lemon juice. Fold in the whipped cream. Finely chop the egg white and add it to the dressing. Just before serving, pour the dressing over the salad.

4 servings

Vanhanaikainensalaatti

Rusks are a good standby in the summertime when it is just too hot to bake bread. They keep well in a tightly covered jar or tin. Most bakeries in Scandinavia have a variety of rusks on hand, and admittedly, most Scandinavians do not make them at home.

In a large mixing bowl, dissolve the yeast in the warm water. Add the brown sugar and let stand for 5 minutes until the yeast foams. Stir in the salt, caraway seeds, milk, rye flour, and whole wheat flour, and beat until smooth.

One cup at a time, add the bread (or all-purpose) flour, beating between each addition, until dough is stiff and will not absorb more flour. Let stand, covered, for 15 minutes.

Sprinkle a work surface with flour, and turn the dough out onto it. Knead, adding flour to prevent stickiness, until the dough is smooth and satiny, about 10 minutes. Knead in the softened butter.

Wash the bowl, grease it, and return the dough to it. Turn the dough over to grease the top of it. Cover and let rise in a warm place until doubled, about 1 hour.

Punch the dough down and turn it out onto an oiled surface. Cut the dough into quarters. Cut each quarter into quarters, then cut each piece in half to make a total of 32 pieces. Shape each piece of dough into a small round ball and place on a floured baking sheet. Cover the baking sheet with a towel and let the dough rise until doubled, about 45 minutes.

Preheat oven to 425°F. Bake the rolls for about 15 minutes, until golden. Cool. Lower oven heat to 300°F. Using 2 forks, split the rolls in half horizontally. Place them on a baking sheet, cut-side up. Bake until golden and dried, about 30 minutes. Remove from the oven and cool on racks. Store the rusks in an airtight container.

64 rusks

CARAWAY RYE RUSKS

2 packages active dry yeast

½ cup warm water (105°F to 115°F)

2 tablespoons brown sugar

1½ teaspoons salt

½ teaspoon caraway seeds

1½ cups milk, scalded and cooled to lukewarm

½ cup dark rye flour

¾ cup whole wheat flour

4 to 4½ cups bread or unbleached all-purpose flour

¼ cup (½ stick) butter, softened

Ruiskorput

SCANDINAVIAN CHEESE TRAY

BUFFETS

EASTER BUFFET

When I asked my Scandinavian friends what they eat for Easter, the reply was, "Eggs, of course!" ∎ Perfect hard-boiled eggs are simple to make: Place the eggs in a nonaluminum saucepan and cover with cold water. Heat to boiling, then reduce the heat and allow the water to barely simmer for 15 minutes. Remove the saucepan from the heat and cool the eggs under cold running water for one minute, to stop the cooking process. ∎ There are really no traditional main dishes associated with Easter in any of the Scandinavian countries. Some people prefer chicken, perhaps because of its association with eggs, and some will choose to bake a salmon, the ubiquitous Scandinavian special-occasion main dish. I include a leg of lamb in this menu because I happen to like lamb for Easter dinner. In Finland, there are two traditional Easter desserts. One is *Mämmi,* a dark baked rye pudding; the other is *Pasha,* a cheesecake-like confection pressed into a carved wooden mold. In Sweden, another kind of cheesecake, called *Ostkaka,* is served. ∎ The Easter table is usually decorated with signs and symbols of new life: fresh flowers, twigs decorated with colored feathers, and brightly painted wooden chicks. I have some friends in Finland who cultivate grass seed in a small flat dish for about two weeks before Easter so that they can use the grass as the centerpiece on their buffet table.

MENU

SALMON TARTARE

EGGS STUFFED WITH HERBS,
MUSTARD, AND CAVIAR

ASPARAGUS WITH
SAFFRON DRESSING

POTATOES STEWED IN CREAM

MARINATED LEG OF LAMB

EASTER PASHA WITH SLICED
FRESH STRAWBERRIES

SWEDISH CHEESECAKE

◉◉◉◉

SALMON TARTARE

In northern Sweden, in the Caledonides mountains, most ski resorts stay open until the end of April, when the skiing is probably the most enjoyable of all thanks to longer, warmer days and lots of good snow. Jan Theisen, a young chef at the Åregården there, serves a delicious variation on the ubiquitous salmon: chopped gravlax mixed with dill and cream and shaped into balls. Although it is wonderful to spread the mixture on bread and eat these little appetizers out of your hand, true Swedish style demands that you use a knife and fork. Please yourself!

With a sharp knife, chop the salmon into pieces no larger than ¼ inch. In a medium-sized bowl, blend the chopped salmon with the fresh dill (or dried dill weed), mayonnaise, sour cream, heavy cream, lemon juice, and pepper.

With a teaspoon dipped in water, or with a small ice cream scoop, form the gravlax mixure into balls. Roll the balls in the dill or parsley. Arrange on a serving plate with lemon wedges, more parsley and/or lettuce, for garnish.

Serve the balls of salmon tartare with the bread.

20 small balls

6 ounces gravlax or lightly salted, sliced salmon, uncooked

1 tablespoon fresh dill, or 2 teaspoons dried dill weed

1 tablespoon mayonnaise

1 tablespoon sour cream

1 tablespoon heavy cream

Few drops lemon juice

Freshly ground white pepper

Finely chopped fresh dill or parsley

Lemon wedges, for garnish

Lettuce, for garnish

Thin slices of fresh or toasted French or rye bread

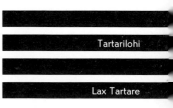

Tartarilohi

Lax Tartare

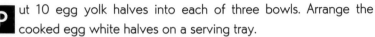

EGGS STUFFED WITH HERBS, MUSTARD, AND CAVIAR

15 hard-boiled eggs, peeled and halved lengthwise

HERB FILLING

¼ cup sour cream

½ teaspoon tarragon

1 tablespoon minced chives

10 pimento-stuffed green olives, for garnish

MUSTARD FILLING

¼ cup sour cream

1 teaspoon Dijon-style mustard

Sliced smoked salmon (*gravlax*), or cooked baby shrimp, for garnish

Fresh dill, for garnish

CAVIAR FILLING

¼ cup sour cream

1 teaspoon lemon juice

2 to 3 tablespoons black and/or red caviar

Thinly sliced lemon, for garnish

Thinly sliced sweet red onion, for garnish

This is a pretty appetizer or first course. You end up with three different fillings for hard-boiled eggs, all of them delicious.

Put 10 egg yolk halves into each of three bowls. Arrange the cooked egg white halves on a serving tray.

To prepare the herb filling, add the sour cream, tarragon, and chives to one of the bowls containing 10 egg yolk halves. Mix until well blended. Spoon the herb filling into 10 of the egg white halves. For garnish, slice the green olives and arrange the slices of one olive on each of the filled egg halves.

To prepare the mustard filling, add the sour cream and mustard to the second bowl of 10 egg yolk halves. Mix until well blended. Spoon the mustard filling into 10 of the egg white halves. Garnish each with a small strip of gravlax or a cooked baby shrimp, and a sprig of fresh dill.

To prepare the caviar filling, add the sour cream and lemon juice to the third bowl of 10 egg yolk halves. Mix until well blended. Spoon the mixture into the remaining 10 egg white halves. Garnish with the black or red caviar, a lemon slice, and a red onion slice.

Cover tray and refrigerate until ready to serve.

10 servings

Fyldte halve aeg

Taytetyt munapuolikkaat

Fylte egg

Fylda Agghälvor

SCANDINAVIAN FEASTS

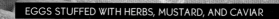

EGGS STUFFED WITH HERBS, MUSTARD, AND CAVIAR

SALMON TARTARE

ASPARAGUS WITH SAFFRON DRESSING

3 pounds fresh asparagus, washed and trimmed

DRESSING

⅓ cup water

¼ teaspoon saffron powder

2 large garlic cloves, minced or crushed through a press

2 egg yolks

1¼ cups olive oil

Salt and freshly ground pepper

This recipe is an adaptation of one created by Chef Erwin Lauterbach of Copenhagen, an advocate of a new, light, Danish cuisine. The combined flavor of saffron and asparagus is refreshing.

ash and trim the asparagus. Plunge into boiling, salted water for 1 to 2 minutes, or just until the asparagus are bright green. Drain well and chill in ice water.

To prepare the dressing, combine the water and saffron powder. Mix in the garlic and egg yolks. Whisk in the olive oil until well blended. Season with salt and pepper.

Pour the dressing over the asparagus, cover, and chill until ready to serve.

10 servings

Aspargessalat i Safron Aeggedressing

Scandinavians love potatoes stewed in cream. As with any classic dish, the recipe varies from region to region, and even from cook to cook. In southern Sweden, for instance, they often sauté finely chopped yellow onions along with the potatoes. I happen to like mine topped with lots of fresh herbs. Serve with almost any roasted or broiled meat or poultry.

Pare and dice the potatoes into ½-inch cubes. Melt the butter in a heavy skillet. Add the potato cubes and sauté them until they are coated with butter and begin to look translucent. Pour the half-and-half over the potatoes. Add the salt. With a spatula, blend the ingredients well. Cover and cook over low heat until the potatoes are soft, about 20 minutes. Sprinkle with the herbs before serving.

10 servings

10 medium-sized (about 1½ pounds) potatoes

2 tablespoons butter

1½ cups half-and-half

1½ teaspoons salt

½ cup finely chopped fresh herbs, such as dill, parsley, or chives, or 2 tablespoons dried herbs

Stuvede Kartofler

Kermassakeitettyperunat

Stuvad Poteter

Stuvad Potatis.

MARINATED LEG OF LAMB

1 (6 to 6½ pound) leg of lamb

2 quarts nonfat buttermilk

2 teaspoons salt

2 tablespoons flour

1 cup water

½ cup sour cream

Salt and pepper to taste

An old Norwegian method of preserving meat is to place it in a container with soured milk, which causes the meat to take on a mellow, sweet-and-sour flavor. This dish is also good served with boiled potatoes and steamed green beans.

Trim the leg of lamb. Place in a nonaluminum pan or in a large, heavy-duty plastic bag. Pour the buttermilk over the lamb and refrigerate for 3 to 4 days. Turn the lamb often if the milk does not cover it completely.

Preheat oven to 325°F.

Remove the lamb from the milk and discard the milk. Dry the meat and rub it with the salt. Place it on a rack in a roasting pan. Pour the water into the bottom of the pan.

Insert a meat thermometer into the thickest part of the roast, being careful not to let the thermometer touch the bone. Roast until the meat reaches 160°F.

Deglaze the roasting pan by adding a little water to it and stirring up the drippings from the bottom of the pan. Strain the drippings and blend in the flour. Cook, stirring, until the gravy is thickened. Add the sour cream, salt, and pepper.

Slice the roast and serve with the gravy.

10 servings

Surstek av Lam

MARINATED LEG OF LAMB

ASPARAGUS WITH SAFFRON DRESSING

POTATOES STEWED IN CREAM

EASTER PASHA

1 cup heavy (whipping) cream

½ cup (1 stick) unsalted butter, at room temperature

1 cup sugar

4 eggs

3 pints ricotta cheese

½ cup sour cream

½ cup minced almonds

½ cup raisins

Fresh fruit, berries, or preserves

Karelians, of Eastern Finland, claim *pasha* as their Easter dessert. It is a mixture of dairy products that are flavored with almonds and raisins, and it is usually served with cloudberry preserves from the Arctic. In Finland, *pasha* is usually made with a fresh cheese called *rahka*. This recipe calls for ricotta. *Pasha* is traditionally baked in a special wooden mold that has the Orthodox Easter symbols carved into the sides so that they are impressed on the dessert when it is unmolded. For the clearest impression of the designs when using a *pasha* mold, use no more than two layers of cheesecloth. If you don't have a *pasha* mold, a clean five- to six-inch clay or plastic flower pot with drain holes on the bottom makes a rather pretty substitute.

In a large metal bowl, combine the cream, butter, sugar, and eggs. With an electric mixer on high speed, beat until light and fluffy. Place the bowl over a pan of boiling water and continue beating the cream mixture until it is thick and light. Remove the bowl from the heat and add the ricotta cheese and sour cream, beating until thick. Blend in the almonds and raisins.

Line a pasha mold (or a clean five- to six-inch flower pot with holes on the bottom) with dampened cheesecloth. Turn the pasha mixture into the lined mold and fold the cheesecloth over the top. Place a one-pound weight (such as a pound of butter or a can of vegetables or fruit) on top. Place in a larger pan (to catch the drippings) and refrigerate for several hours or overnight, draining off the liquids several times, until the pasha is firm. Before serving, unmold the pasha onto a serving plate. Serve with fresh fruit, berries, or preserves.

10 servings

Pääsiäispasha

SWEDISH CHEESECAKE

Swedes make this ancient variety of cheesecake in the springtime after the dairy cows have calved. The cows' "new milk" or colostrum milk has a natural rennet in it, which causes the milk to set when heated. It is not easy (even in Sweden) to get colostrum milk today, so I have revised this recipe accordingly: Instead of cheese made with colostrum milk, I use ricotta with excellent results. I enjoyed this memorable cheesecake at Tanum's Gestgifveri, a Swedish countryside inn in the village of Tanumshede, prepared by Christian Giertta, the inn's talented chef.

Preheat oven to 350°F.

In a large mixing bowl, combine the ricotta cheese, flour, lemon juice, eggs, sugar, and cream. Mix with a whisk until well blended. Add the almonds. Turn into a lightly greased 2-quart baking dish.

Bake for 1 hour, or until the cake is set. Remove from the oven. Serve while still slightly warm or at room temperature. Cut into squares or wedges to serve.

10 to 12 servings

1 (30-ounce) carton ricotta cheese, about 3½ cups

½ cup flour

¼ cup lemon juice

4 eggs

¼ cup sugar

2 cups heavy (whipping) cream

½ cup finely chopped almonds

Smålandsk ostkaka

EASTER PASHA

SWEDISH CHEESECAKE

CANDLEMAKING BUFFET

Around the first of December, the new ecclesiastical year begins, and the season that follows until Christmas is called Advent. In the old days, candles were made on the Saturday before the first Sunday in Advent, not only for Christmas but to light the household through the long, dark days of winter. Candlemaking is an activity in which the whole family can get involved. Candle wax is heated in a tall, narrow container that is placed in a kettle of hot water. Wicks are dipped into the hot wax, building up the candles to about an inch in diameter. The candles need to cool off and harden between dippings, providing convenient breaks for snacking. ▪ Today, of course, candlemaking is done just for fun, and sometimes the preparation of an Advent wreath to hold the candles replaces the traditional Advent candlemaking. The Advent wreath holds four Advent candles, decorated with green-leafed lingonberry twigs dug up from under the snow. On the morning of the first Sunday in Advent, the family gathers for an Advent breakfast and lights the first Advent candle. On each of the subsequent Sundays of Advent an additional candle is lit and on Christmas, a fifth candle is lit and placed in the center of the wreath. ▪ Many of the items on this menu can be purchased at the supermarket. A number of Scandinavian cheeses are available in American markets, including Jarlsberg, Nokkleost, Havarti, Bondost, Danablu and Sagablu, and Gjetost. A good sampling of them, along with the fresh sliced vegetables, fruit, and walnuts makes a simple feast to prepare. All you need do is arrange them on a tray.

MENU

SCANDINAVIAN CHEESE TRAY

THREE-GRAIN ALMOND HARDTACK

RYE CRISPBREADS

TOMATO, ONION, AND
CUCUMBER SLICES

GREEN, RED, AND YELLOW BELL
PEPPER SLICES

RADISHES, GRAPES, WALNUT HALVES

TOMATO POTATO SOUP

SWEDISH FILBERT CAKE

This nutty crispbread goes well with cheese. To achieve the characteristic pebbly texture on the top of the bread, you will need a special hardtack rolling pin, which can be found in stores that specialize in Scandinavian foods and tools.

Preheat oven to 350°F. Lightly grease four 11-by-17-inch baking sheets.

In a large bowl, cream the shortening, butter, and sugar, until smooth. Add the all-purpose and rye flours, rolled oats, almonds, salt, and baking soda, and mix until crumbly and blended. Stir the lemon juice (or vinegar) into the milk, then blend into the dry mixture, until a stiff dough forms. Divide the dough into four equal parts. Using a hardtack or standard rolling pin, roll out one part all the way to the edges on each baking sheet. If you do not have a hardtack rolling pin, pierce the dough all over with a fork. Score into 2-by-4-inch pieces, leaving the dough in place. Bake for 25 minutes or until lightly browned and crisp. Allow to cool on baking sheets, then remove and store in an airtight container.

112 2-by-4-inch squares

½ cup vegetable shortening

¼ cup (½ stick) butter, at room temperature

½ cup sugar

3 cups all-purpose flour

1 cup dark rye flour

1 cup rolled oats, finely pulverized

1 cup unblanched almonds, pulverized

1½ teaspoons salt

1 teaspoon baking soda

1 tablespoon lemon juice or white vinegar

1½ cups milk

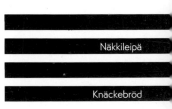

Näkkileipä

Knäckebröd

TOMATO POTATO SOUP

1 pound (4 or 5 large) fresh tomatoes, peeled

6 medium-sized potatoes, pared and cubed

4 medium-sized onions, peeled and diced

8 cups chicken broth

⅓ cup all-purpose flour

Salt and pepper

2 cups heavy (whipping) cream

Chopped parsley, for garnish

This pale pink, creamy soup is fast and easy to make. It can be served hot or cold.

Combine the tomatoes, potatoes, onions, and broth in a 4- to 5-quart pot. Heat to simmering and cook until the vegetables are tender, 25 to 30 minutes. Scoop the vegetables into a blender and process until puréed (you will have to do this in batches). When you purée the final batch, add the flour while the motor is still running, blending it well. Return all of the purée to the pot and heat to simmering, stirring, until slightly thickened. Season with salt and pepper. Add the cream just before serving. Garnish with the chopped parsley.

12 servings

Kartoffelsuppe

Tomattiperunakeitto

Potetsuppe

Potatissoppa

SWEDISH FILBERT CAKE

This cake can be made with pecans or walnuts instead of filberts, and looks lovely when baked in a fancy tube pan. Top with whipped cream and preserved or fresh fruits.

Preheat oven to 350°F. Butter a 9-inch tube pan and dust with cookie or bread crumbs.

In a medium-sized bowl, beat the eggs and sugar until light and fluffy. Pulverize the nuts in a food processor, then fold them into the egg mixture. Combine the flour and baking powder and sift it through a strainer into the cake mixture. Blend in the melted butter and cream. Pour the batter into the prepared pan and bake for 50 minutes, or until a toothpick inserted in the center of the cake comes out clean.

12 slices

4 eggs

1⅓ cups sugar

2 cups filberts

1⅓ cups flour

2 teaspoons baking powder

½ cup (1 stick) butter, melted

1 cup light cream

Hasselnötskaka

NAME DAY FEAST IN FINLAND

Throughout Scandinavia, one's name day—the day honoring the saint after whom you were named—is often celebrated in place of or in addition to one's birthday. An American exchange student I know came home after her year in Finland all excited because, she said, "You get to celebrate two birthdays a year there." The last time I visited Finland, I was invited to my friend Kaija's name day celebration. She shares her name day, November 25th, with all those whose names derive from Saint Katherine—typically Karin, Carina, Katja, and Kaisa, as well as names less typically Scandinavian, such as Kathleen. These celebrations very often feature personal gifts, for instance, poems specially written for the occasion, songs and other musical interludes, flowers, and, of course, good food and a celebratory glass of champagne. ■ For her guests, Kaija set out a seafood buffet consisting of an assortment of shrimp and fish pâtés balanced by marinated mushrooms and a number of colorful vegetable salads. The single hot dish was Jansson's Temptation, a delectable traditional combination of potatoes and Swedish anchovies baked with cream. For those who wanted something sweet at the end of the meal, there were not one, but two, chocolate cakes, but in this menu I only give the recipe for one of them.

MENU

SALMON PATE

SALMON AND WHITEFISH MOUSSE

MARINATED MUSHROOMS

DILLED SHRIMP

JANSSON'S TEMPTATION

CHAMPAGNE, SPARKLING WHITE
WINE, OR SPICED WHITE GRAPE JUICE

THE PROFESSOR'S
CHOCOLATE CAKE

COFFEE

◉◉◉◉

JANSSON'S TEMPTATION

SALMON PATE

½ pound fresh salmon, skinned and
boned

2 tablespoons butter

½ pound cooked smoked salmon,
skinned and boned (not cured
salmon, gravlax, or lox)

1 cup heavy (whipping) cream

3 tablespoons chopped fresh dill

This delicate pâté of fresh and smoked salmon is best served in a
pretty terrine. To serve, scoop out the pâté with a wooden paddle and
spread it on croutons, crackers, or thin slices of French bread.

In a heavy skillet, over low heat, sauté the fresh salmon in the
butter, just until cooked through, about 10 minutes. Chill.
Crumble the smoked salmon into the work bowl of a food processor
fitted with a steel blade. Process until puréed. With the motor still
running, add the cream. Add the cooked, chilled salmon and process
until smooth. Blend in half the dill. Turn into a serving dish or tureen.
Sprinkle with the remaining dill. Chill and serve.

Approximately 2 ½ cups

Lakspostej

Savukalapate

Lakspate

Röktlaxpate

Fish mousse (or fish pudding), traditionally made from Norwegian codfish, is one of the finest dishes in Scandinavian cuisine. In the old days, the beating that accounts for its light texture was done with a wooden spoon, but today the food processor does all the work.

Combine the fish cubes in a stainless steel bowl. Add the wine and lemon juice and marinate for 2 to 24 hours.

Press the fish through the fine disk of a meat grinder three times, or process in a food processor fitted with a steel blade until puréed. Place the fish back in the bowl and chill for 1 hour.

In the large bowl of an electric mixer set at high speed, beat the chilled fish until light in texture. Gradually beat in the eggs, egg whites, salt, white pepper, potato flour (or cornstarch), and cream, until the mixture's texture is very light and fluffy.

Preheat oven to 400°F. Butter a 2-quart loaf pan or terrine. Turn the fish mixture into the pan (or terrine). Cover with waxed paper, then with foil. Place the pan (or terrine) into a larger pan and add enough boiling water to come halfway up the pan (or terrine) containing the mousse.

Bake for 1½ hours, or until the fish is cooked through.

To make the caviar sauce, in a small bowl, blend together the sour cream, lemon juice, and caviar.

Remove from the oven and unmold onto a serving plate. Garnish with fresh dill sprigs and serve hot or chilled with the caviar sauce.

Approximately 18 ½-inch-thick slices

1½ pounds salmon fillet, skinned, deboned, and cubed

¾ pound whitefish fillet, skinned, deboned, and cubed

¼ cup dry white wine

2 tablespoons fresh lemon juice

3 eggs plus 2 egg whites

2 teaspoons salt

¼ teaspoon freshly ground white pepper

1½ tablespoons potato flour or cornstarch

2 cups heavy (whipping) cream

Fresh dill sprigs, for garnish

CAVIAR SAUCE

1 cup sour cream

2 tablespoons lemon juice

¼ cup (2 ounces) fresh whitefish caviar or red salmon caviar

Laksbudding

Lohimureke

Lakspudding

Laxfars

DILLED SHRIMP

¼ cup salt

⅓ cup sugar

1 large bunch fresh dill, or ¼ cup dried
dill weed

2 pounds medium shrimp (30 to 40 per
pound)

MARINADE

2 tablespoons salad oil

1 tablespoon white wine vinegar

1 tablespoon minced fresh dill, or 2
teaspoons dried dill weed

¼ teaspoon salt

Dash pepper

Fresh dill sprigs or heads, for garnish

These shrimp are served cold, but a special marinade keeps them moist, while adding complementary flavor. Although I like to serve the shrimp with a dipping sauce, Scandinavians generally serve them without one.

Boil 2 quarts of water in a deep pot. Add the salt, sugar, and dill. Drop in the shrimp and boil until they turn bright pink, about 3 to 5 minutes. Remove the shrimp from the water and let cool for about 5 minutes. Drain, peel, and devein them. Place the shrimp in a large bowl.

In a small bowl, combine the salad oil, vinegar, dill, salt, and pepper. Pour over the shrimp and mix until well coated. Cover and chill for 2 to 4 hours, or overnight.

When you are ready to serve, turn the shrimp out onto a shallow serving platter. Garnish with sprigs or heads of dill.

Approximately 12 appetizer servings

Rejer

Keitetty Katkaravut

Koktreke

DILLED SHRIMP

SALMON PATE

SALMON AND WHITEFISH MOUSSE

JANSSON'S TEMPTATION

6 medium-sized (about 1 pound)
potatoes

2 large yellow onions

1 (4½-ounce) tin Swedish anchovy
fillets (14 to 16 fillets)

1 to 1½ cups heavy (whipping) cream

2 tablespoons dry bread crumbs

1 tablespoon butter, melted

You will always find Jansson's Temptation on the smorgasbord in Sweden, and it is often served as a luncheon or midnight dish. Its popularity has spread to Finland and Norway as well.

To get the right flavor in this dish, you must use Swedish anchovies, which are cured in a slightly sweet brine and are not as salty as common anchovies. You can find them in Scandinavian specialty stores in jars and flat tins, but buy the fillets rather than the whole little fish or you'll have to clean and fillet them yourself. If you cannot find Swedish anchovies, substitute a package of lightly smoked salmon or lox, but of course, it will not be the same.

Preheat oven to 425°F. Butter a 2-quart shallow baking dish. Peel, rinse, and cut the potatoes into thin strips that are no thicker than ¼-inch. Peel the onions and discard the ends. Cut the onion in two, lengthwise. With the cut side face down, slice the onions lengthwise into ¼-inch strips.

Spread the onions and anchovies into the prepared dish. Cover with the potato strips. Add just enough cream to cover the potatoes. Mix together the bread crumbs and melted butter, then sprinkle over the potato mixture. Bake for 45 to 50 minutes, until the potatoes are tender and the top is browned.

6 servings

Jansonin Kiusaus

Janssons Fristelse

Jansson's Frestelse

THE PROFESSOR'S CHOCOLATE CAKE

Perhaps the reason this dessert is called the "professor's" chocolate cake is that it is not an old-fashioned, country-style cake, but rather one that might appeal to so-called educated tastes. The cake should be gooey on the inside. To gild the lily, it can be served with whipped cream, although I like it unadorned.

Preheat oven to 350°F. Butter and flour a 9-inch cake pan, preferably one with removable sides.

In a small saucepan, over low heat, melt the chocolate, butter, and sugar. Set aside to cool.

In a medium-sized bowl, beat the egg whites until stiff.

Stir the egg yolks into the cooled chocolate mixture. Add the flour, nuts, and instant coffee. Fold in the egg whites. Pour into the baking pan and bake for 35 to 40 minutes. To garnish, dust with the powdered sugar. To serve, cut into wedges.

12 wedges

6 ounces semisweet chocolate

¾ cup (1½ sticks) butter

¾ cup sugar

3 eggs, separated

⅓ cup flour

¾ cup chopped filberts, walnuts, or pecans

1 tablespoon instant coffee

Powdered sugar, for garnish

Professorin Suklaakakku

Professorns Chokladkaka

FINNISH THREE-MEAT RAGOUT

MASHED POTATO AND RUTABAGA CASSEROLE

KARELIAN RYE-CRUSTED PASTRIES WITH EGG BUTTER

KARELIAN COUNTRY BUFFET

In the old days in Karelia, located in the easternmost province of Finland, fresh baked goods were prepared daily. ■ The kitchen stove, which was a mammoth construction of stone or bricks, was fired up each morning and when the oven was at its hottest, cooks would bake rye-crusted, rice-, barley-, or potato-filled pastries. As the oven cooled to the lower temperatures, loaves of bread, cakes, and cookies were baked. Last of all, a pot of rice or barley, and a stew, called *paisti,* made with three kinds of meat, were placed into the oven to cook slowly as the oven cooled during the night. The next morning, the baked rice or barley was served for breakfast and the leftovers were made into special pastries called *piirakka.* ■ All of the items on this menu can be found throughout Finland in restaurants that feature native cuisine. In eastern Finland, at the Bomba, a charming country inn made up of restored old buildings, the restaurant serves only authentic Karelian food. There is a healthy, earthy quality to the foods there and in this menu: whole grain pie crusts, slow-cooked ragout, mushrooms, potatoes, and rutabagas. Even the dessert tastes healthy.

MENU

**KARELIAN RYE-CRUSTED PASTRIES
WITH EGG BUTTER**

FINNISH THREE-MEAT RAGOUT

**MASHED POTATO AND
RUTABAGA CASSEROLE**

**MUSHROOM AND
SOUR CREAM SALAD**

APPLE CRANBERRY PUDDING

◉◉◉◉

KARELIAN RYE-CRUSTED PASTRIES WITH EGG BUTTER

FILLING

2 cups water

1 cup uncooked rice

2 cups milk

Salt

CRUST

½ cup water

1 teaspoon salt

1 cup rye flour

¼ cup all-purpose flour

Barley, a grain native to northern climates, was probably the first filling that was ever used in these little pies. As soon as Scandinavians began growing potatoes, which were not introduced until the 1600s, Karelian cooks started to use them in their *piirakka*, and today potatoes are a favorite filling (you can use about 4 cups of mashed potatoes seasoned with salt and pepper to fill the pastries in this recipe). Rice, though it has never been native to Scandinavia, is the third classic filling, and the one given here.

Rather than rolling out the dough for each individual pie, sometimes I roll the dough as if for cookies, cut out three-inch rounds, and then fill and crimp the edges to make the oval shape. Most Finns like to wrap the pastries in waxed paper so that the crusts will soften. I prefer them hot and crisp.

For the filling, in a saucepan, combine the water and rice. Bring to a boil. Stir, cover, and cook over low heat for 20 minutes, stirring occasionally. Add the milk, cover, and continue cooking until the milk is completely absorbed and the rice is soft and creamy. Season with salt.

Preheat oven to 500°F. Line a baking sheet with parchment paper.

Karjalan Piirakka ja Munavoi

To prepare the pastry, in a medium-sized bowl, combine the water, salt, and rye and white flours to make a stiff dough. Shape the dough into a log and cut into 16 parts. Shape each part into a round. On a lightly floured board, roll out each round into a 6-inch circle.

Spread about 3 tablespoons of filling evenly on each round. Fold two opposite edges of the pastry over the filling and crimp the edges of the dough toward the center to make an oval-shaped pastry, allowing about ½-inch of the crust to overlap the filling and leaving the center of the filling exposed. Place on the prepared baking sheet.

In a small bowl, stir together the melted butter and hot milk and brush on the pastries. Bake for 10 to 15 minutes, brushing once during baking, until the pastries are golden on the edges. Remove from the oven and brush again.

To prepare the egg butter, in a small bowl, cream the butter. Stir in the eggs. Season with the white pepper and ground ginger, if desired. Serve the egg butter at room temperature.

Cool the pastries and serve with the egg butter.

16 pastries, 1 cup egg butter

BASTE

½ cup (1 stick) butter, melted

½ cup hot milk

EGG BUTTER

½ cup (1 stick) butter, at room temperature

2 hard-boiled eggs, chopped

Pinch freshly ground white pepper (optional)

Pinch ground ginger (optional)

FINNISH THREE-MEAT RAGOUT

1 pound lean lamb, shoulder or leg

1 pound lean pork, shoulder or leg

1 pound lean beef round

2½ teaspoons salt

1 teaspoon whole allspice

½ teaspoon whole white peppercorns

6 large white onions, cut into ¼-inch-thick slices

Chopped fresh parsley

This is one of my favorite meat dishes because it is so tasty and so simple to make. I choose lean but rather tough shoulder or leg cuts for their well-developed flavor. Layered in an enamelled cast-iron pot and covered tightly, the meat and onions stew to tender succulence in about 5 hours, and are then spooned over mashed potatoes or a combination of mashed potatoes and rutabagas. This recipe makes a large amount, but you can freeze what is left over.

Preheat oven to 300°F. Cut the meat into 1-inch cubes. In an enamelled, cast-iron pot or other deep ovenproof casserole, layer the meat, salt, allspice, white peppercorns, and onion. Cover tightly. Bake for 5 hours, or until the meat is very tender.

Sprinkle with chopped fresh parsley and serve over mashed potatoes or mashed potatoes and rutabagas.

12 servings

Karjalan Paisti

MASHED POTATO AND RUTABAGA CASSEROLE

I like the creamy color of mashed rutabagas together with potatoes in this casserole. It can be assembled a day in advance, if desired.

Put the potatoes in a large pot and cover them with water. Add 1 teaspoon salt for each quart of water. Heat to boiling and cook for 20 to 25 minutes, until the potatoes are tender. Drain, peel, and mash the cooked potatoes.

Meanwhile, pare the rutabaga and cut it into 1-inch pieces. Place in a saucepan, cover with water, and bring to a boil. Simmer until tender, 25 to 30 minutes. Drain, mash, and add the cooked rutabaga to the potatoes. Beat with an electric mixer until the potatoes and rutabagas are smooth and fluffy. Beat in the flour, eggs, salt, and milk (or cream).

Preheat oven to 350°F. Butter a 3-quart shallow baking dish. Turn the mixture into the dish. Using a spoon, spread out the mixture, making indentations in the top of the casserole. Dot with the butter and sprinkle with the bread crumbs. Bake uncovered for 1 hour, or until lightly browned.

12 servings

2 pounds thin-skinned boiling potatoes

Salt

1 pound (about 1 medium) rutabaga

¼ cup flour

2 eggs

2 teaspoons salt

½ to 1 cup hot milk or light cream

1 tablespoon butter

¼ cup fine dry bread crumbs

Peruna ja lanttulaatikko

MUSHROOM AND SOUR CREAM SALAD

4 cups water

2 teaspoons salt

2 pounds mushrooms, cleaned and sliced

1 cup sour cream

1 teaspoon sugar

2 teaspoons white vinegar or lemon juice

4 tablespoons grated white onion

Crisp lettuce, for garnish

Finns use chanterelles or other wild mushrooms to make this salad, but the standard supermarket variety will work well also. Serve in small spoonfuls.

In a large saucepan, bring the water and 1 teaspoon salt to a boil. Drop in the mushrooms and cook for 3 to 4 minutes. Drain, pat dry, and allow to cool. Finely chop the cooled mushrooms and drain them again. Turn into a bowl and sprinkle with the remaining teaspoon of salt. Turn into a colander or strainer, and drain for 1 hour. It is not necessary to refrigerate the mushrooms while draining.

In a small bowl, stir together the sour cream, sugar, vinegar (or lemon juice), and onion. Combine in a bowl with the chopped mushrooms. Cover and chill to allow flavors to blend.

Serve on a platter lined with crisp lettuce, or on individual plates lined with lettuce.

12 servings

Sienisalaatti

SCANDINAVIAN FEASTS

Puddings made with clear juices are a popular dessert in Finland. In this recipe, apple slices are poached in cranberry juice. Then the juice is thickened and served over the cooked apple.

In a 3-quart saucepan, heat the cranberry juice and sugar. Add the apple slices and simmer for 10 minutes, or until the apples are tender. With a slotted spoon, transfer the apples to a dessert bowl.

Mix the potato starch (or cornstarch) with the apple juice (or water). Reheat the cranberry juice to a boil and slowly add the starch mixture, stirring with a whisk. Reduce the heat and simmer until the juice thickens and becomes transparent. Pour the juice over the cooked apple. Cover and let cool. Serve warm or chilled with whipped cream or light cream.

12 servings

6 cups bottled cranberry juice

½ to ¾ cup sugar, depending on sweetness of juice

4 Granny Smith apples, pared, cored, and sliced crosswise

½ cup potato starch or cornstarch

⅔ cup apple juice or cold water

Whipped cream or light cream

Omenakarpalokiisseli

DANISH SMØRREBRØD BUFFET

SCANDINAVIAN FEASTS

A DANISH SMØRREBRØD

Smørrebrød is very often a Saturday evening meal in Denmark, and, like a patchwork quilt, it is frequently made of leftovers. Sliced cooked meats, such as roast chicken, beef, or pork roast or chops, sautéed apples and onions, smoked salmon, boiled shrimp, cucumber salad, curried vegetables, lettuce, tomato—the list goes on and on. ■ Danes like to butter their bread generously. In fact, the literal translation of smørrebrød is buttered bread. Ida Davidson, the "Smørrebrød Queen" of Denmark gave me just one other rule concerning these sandwiches: The topping should cover the bread completely and any meat should hang over the edges of the bread by about an inch or so. Not only the Danes, but all Scandinavians, consider sandwiches to be knife-and-fork fare, as opposed to finger food, with toppings piled on a single slice of bread. ■ The dozen smørrebrød recipes here are a sampler from the menu at Ida Davidson's restaurant in Copenhagen, which, I was told, is the most extensive smørrebrød menu in the world: It includes an amazing list of 177 different sandwiches! To organize a buffet menu, select three or four contrasting types of smørrebrød and plan on a total of about three smørrebrød per person. For convenience, they can be made ahead of time, covered, and refrigerated. These sandwiches make a colorful presentation, perfect for easy, buffet-style entertaining. Serve them with Danish beer and schnapps, or tea and coffee, or soft drinks.

MENU

THE VETERINARIAN'S BREAKFAST

THE VETERINARIAN'S SUPPER

THE GOLDEN SUNRISE

THE PRAWN PYRAMID

THE HANS CHRISTIAN ANDERSEN

THE PER HENRIKSEN

BEEF TARTARE AND SHRIMP

POOR MAN'S BEEF TARTARE

BACON AND CAMEMBERT

EGG AND CAVIAR

MODERN ROAST BEEF

THE ELECTRICIAN'S SUPPER

THE VETERINARIAN'S BREAKFAST

1 teaspoon butter

1 slice rye bread

1 slice liver pâté

2 tablespoons chilled beef consommé aspic, chopped

4 thin slices Danish salami

3 sweet onion rings

1 sprig fresh dill, for garnish

This is named after a Copenhagen veterinarian, or *Dyrlaegen,* who ordered it every morning on his way to work.

Spread the butter to the edges of the rye bread. Top with the liver pâté and beef consommé aspic. Arrange the salami so that the outer edges completely hide the bread and the meat overlaps in the center of the sandwich. Arrange the onion rings on top and place a sprig of fresh dill in the center of the onion rings.

1 serving

THE VETERINARIAN'S SUPPER

1 teaspoon butter

1 slice rye bread

1 slice liver pâté

1 teaspoon lard (optional)

1 tablespoon crisp pork cracklings or bacon bits

2 tablespoons beef consommé aspic, diced

4 thin slices salted cooked beef

3 to 4 rings sweet onion

1 sprig dill, for garnish

The *same Dyrlaegen* (veterinarian) stopped into the Davidson *Smørrebrød* Shop every evening for his supper. This is the combination he would then order.

Spread the butter to the edges of the rye bread. Top with the liver pâté. To be authentic, spread the liver pâté with lard, then sprinkle with pork cracklings (or bacon bits). Top the cracklings (or bacon bits) with the beef consommé aspic. Arrange the cooked beef so that the outer edges completely hide the bread and the meat overlaps in the center of the sandwich. Arrange the onion rings on top and place a sprig of fresh dill in the center of the onion rings.

1 serving

♡

The combination of blue cheese, tomato, and egg yolk is a Danish favorite, but you can substitute a tablespoon of hollandaise sauce for the egg yolk. When using an egg shell for garnish, before cracking it, wash the egg in soapy water, rinse and pat dry.

Spread the butter to the edges of the bread. Arrange the cheese slices to completely hide the bread. Place the tomato slice on top. Place the egg yolk in a half of a washed egg shell, or spoon hollandaise sauce into the shell and nest it on top of the tomato slice.

1 serving

❋

This *smørrebrød* is often served in a "do-it-yourself" fashion. When serving to a group, first pass the bread and butter, and then a bowlful of shrimp.

Spread the butter to the edges of the bread. Arrange the shrimp in rows on top of the bread. Garnish with a lemon wedge (optional) and a sprig of dill. Drizzle with melted butter, if desired.

1 serving

THE GOLDEN SUNRISE

1 teaspoon butter

1 slice French bread

4 thin slices blue cheese

1 slice tomato

1 raw egg yolk, or 1 tablespoon hollandaise sauce, in a half of an egg shell

THE PRAWN PYRAMID

1 teaspoon butter

1 slice French bread

¼ pound small, cooked shrimp

1 wedge lemon (optional), for garnish

1 sprig dill, for garnish

Melted butter (optional)

THE HANS CHRISTIAN ANDERSEN

1 teaspoon butter

1 slice rye bread

4 slices crisp cooked bacon

1 slice liver pâté

2 tablespoons (1 strip) chilled
   consommé aspic

4 thin slices tomato

1 tablespoon grated fresh horseradish

Chopped parsley

The following was one of Hans Christian Andersen's favorites.

Spread the butter to the edges of the rye bread. Arrange the bacon over the bread, then top with a slice of liver pâté and a strip of aspic. Overlap the tomato slices alongside the aspic. Spoon on the horseradish and sprinkle with parsley.

1 serving

THE PER HENRIKSEN

1 teaspoon butter

1 slice rye bread

2 hard-boiled eggs, cut into thin
   wedges

1 tomato, cut into thin slices

5 thin slices cucumber

2 tablespoons chopped sweet onion

1 tablespoon mayonnaise

1 raw egg yolk, or 1 tablespoon
   hollandaise sauce, in a half of
   an egg shell

1 sprig fresh dill, for garnish

Nothing is known about Per Henriksen except that he was a regular at the Davidson *Smørrebrød* Shop, and he always requested this excellent combination.

Spread the butter to the edges of the rye bread. Arrange the egg wedges around the outside edges of the bread. Arrange the tomato slices inside the ring of egg wedges, then top with the cucumber and onion. Top with the mayonnaise. Fill a well-washed and rinsed half of an egg shell with an egg yolk (or hollandaise sauce) and position it on top of the mayonnaise. Garnish the mayonnaise with dill.

1 serving

BEEF TARTARE AND SHRIMP

The shrimp radiates in four lines, from the center toward each corner, to make the sign of the Union Jack.

Spread the butter to the edges of the rye bread. On a flat platter, using a spatula, mash the beef into a flattened cake. As a guide, place the rye bread on top of the meat and straighten out the edges of the beef so that they extend about an inch beyond the edges of the bread. With a spatula, scrape up the beef and place it on top of the bread, making sure that the beef completely covers the bread and the edges are straight. Arrange the shrimp in 4 lines, each one extending from the center to one corner of the *smørrebrød*. Put the egg yolk (or hollandaise sauce) into a well-washed and rinsed half of an egg shell and position it in the center of the *smørrebrød*.

1 serving

1 teaspoon butter

1 slice rye bread

3 ounces freshly ground beef sirloin

16 freshly cooked tiny shrimp or prawns

1 raw egg yolk, or 1 tablespoon hollandaise sauce, in a half of an egg shell

POOR MAN'S BEEF TARTARE

A raw egg yolk becomes the sauce for this interesting combination of vegetables. If you wish, however, you can fill the egg shell with a freshly made hollandaise sauce.

Spread the butter to the edges of the rye bread. Arrange the tomato slices so that they completely cover the bread. Top with the onion, capers, horseradish, and parsley. Fill a well-washed and rinsed half of an egg shell with an egg yolk (or hollandaise sauce) and position on top of the sandwich.

1 serving

1 teaspoon butter

1 slice rye bread

8 to 10 thin slices of a small tomato

2 tablespoons chopped onion

1 tablespoon capers

2 tablespoons freshly ground horseradish

1 teaspoon chopped parsley

1 raw egg yolk, or 1 tablespoon hollandaise sauce, in a half of an egg shell

BACON AND CAMEMBERT

1 teaspoon butter

1 slice rye bread

4 slices crisp bacon

4 thin slices Camembert or Brie cheese

1 small tomato, cut into 6 wedges

4 strips green bell pepper

Slice the Camembert when it is still chilled, but, for the best flavor, allow the sandwich to come to room temperature before eating.

Spread the butter to the edges of the rye bread. Arrange the bacon to cover the bread, then arrange the cheese over it. Arrange the tomato wedges over the cheese, then top with the bell pepper. Allow the sandwich to come to room temperature before serving.

1 serving

EGG AND CAVIAR

1 teaspoon butter

1 slice French bread

2 hard-boiled eggs, each cut into
    6 wedges

2 tablespoons black caviar

1 sprig fresh dill, for garnish

Hard-boiled eggs and caviar are a wonderful combination. For an elegant appetizer, cut the bread slices into quarters before adding the toppings.

Spread the butter to the edges of the bread. Arrange the egg wedges to completely cover the bread. Spoon on the caviar and garnish with the dill.

1 serving

MODERN ROAST BEEF

This popular open-faced sandwich is offered in cafeterias and cafés throughout Scandinavia.

Spread the butter to the edges of the rye bread. Arrange the meat so it completely covers the bread and overlaps in the center. Arrange the egg wedges on one half of the bread and the tomato slices on the other. Spoon the crispy fried onions down the center.

1 serving

1 teaspoon butter

1 slice rye bread

2 thinly sliced pieces of rare roast beef

1 hard-boiled egg, cut into 6 wedges

4 slices fresh tomato

4 tablespoons canned crispy fried onions

THE ELECTRICIAN'S SUPPER

An electrician ordered this sandwich at the Davidson *Smørrebrød* Shop so frequently, it became known as The Electrician's Supper.

Spread the butter to the edges of the rye bread. Arrange the meat slices to completely cover the bread. Arrange the warm onion and apple slices on top of the meat. Spoon the pork gravy (or mustard vinaigrette) on top.

To prepare the mustard vinaigrette, in a small bowl, whisk together the mustard, vinegar, and oil. Season to taste with the salt and pepper.

1 serving

1 teaspoon butter

1 slice rye bread

6 thin slices cooked, cold pork chops

1 small onion, thinly sliced and sautéed

1 small apple, pared, cored, sliced, and sautéed

4 tablespoons leftover, warmed-up pork gravy, or 2 tablespoons mustard vinaigrette

MUSTARD VINAIGRETTE

1½ teaspoons strong dark mustard

1½ teaspoons red wine vinegar

1 tablespoon salad oil

Salt and pepper

DANISH CRACKLING ROAST PORK

SWEET-AND-SOUR RED CABBAGE

SUGAR-BROWNED POTATOES

DINNERS

DANISH CONFIRMATION FEAST

For Lutherans—who make up the predominant denomination in Scandinavia—confirmation is the celebration of passage into adulthood for young boys and girls. It comes after intense study of the articles of faith, and at the rite of confirmation, each boy and girl "reconfirms" his or her own baptism, which occurred at infancy. ▪ Danish families attach great importance to this occasion and celebrate it with a dinner or a party either at home or in a restaurant. All the proud relatives are invited, and to fulfill one of the first assignments of adult life, the confirmand chooses the menu. ▪ Although technically anything in the world could be selected, most will choose this traditional feast. Throughout Denmark, the menu is remarkably identical. It starts with *klarsuppe,* a rich beef broth with tiny meatballs and dumplings. Following that is a pork roast, baked so that the fat on the roast is crisp, accompanied by both white and sugar-browned potatoes and succulent cooked red cabbage. Danish Ice Cream Cake is the most popular dessert. Sometimes *kransekake* (see pages 74–76), the festive almond wreath cake, or ginger cookies are served with it.

MENU

MEATBALL AND DUMPLING SOUP

SUGAR-BROWNED POTATOES

DANISH CRACKLING ROAST PORK

SWEET-AND-SOUR RED CABBAGE

ICE CREAM CAKE

SPICY GINGER COOKIES
(SEE PAGE 241)

◎◎◎◎

This soup is served on almost every special occasion in Denmark, sometimes as a *Skorup-Af-Suppe,* a nightcap signaling the end of a party. Food historian Huggo Jensen said, "Frankly, it's the only way to get rid of people when the party is over."

To prepare the meatballs, in a food processor fitted with a steel blade, process the meat and onion until very fine and light. Or, put through a food grinder three times, until very fine. Add the salt, pepper, and allspice. In a separate bowl, stir together the flour and milk to make a paste, then add it to the meat mixture. Add the egg white and mix well. Let stand for at least 30 minutes before continuing so that the liquids are absorbed.

Bring about 2 inches of water to boiling in a skillet. Add 1 teaspoon of salt per quart of water.

Using the tip of a teaspoon, shape the meat mixture into 40 small balls. Drop the balls into the boiling water and boil for 4 to 5 minutes, until cooked. Lift the meatballs out of the water with a perforated spoon. Place the meatballs in a sieve or strainer, rinse with cold water, and let meatballs drip until dry. The meatballs can be made a day ahead of time, then warmed again in the soup.

Continued on following page

MEATBALLS

½ **pound ground meat, pork, veal, beef, or turkey**

½ **cup chopped onion**

1 **teaspoon salt**

¼ **teaspoon pepper**

⅛ **teaspoon ground allspice**

3 **tablespoons flour**

3 **tablespoons milk**

1 **egg white, lightly beaten**

Salt

Klarsuppe med Boller

Continued from preceding page

DUMPLINGS

½ cup (1 stick) butter

1 cup water

1 teaspoon salt

1 cup flour

3 eggs

Salt

BROTH

2 quarts well-flavored beef consommé

½ cup diced carrots, cooked

½ cup baby peas, cooked

Chervil, for garnish

To prepare the dumplings, in a saucepan, bring the butter, water, and salt to a boil. Add the flour all at once, stirring vigorously. When the mixture is smooth, shiny, and thick enough to make a ball that leaves the sides of the pan, remove from the heat and cool for 10 minutes. Mix in the eggs, one at a time, beating well.

Bring about 2 inches of water to a simmer in a skillet. Add 1 teaspoon of salt per quart of water.

Using two teaspoons, shape the dough into 40 small balls. Drop the dough balls gently into the simmering water. Bring the water to a boil, and as soon as it begins to boil, add a small amount of cold water. Repeat the procedure of bringing the water to a boil and adding a small amount of cold water three times. The dumplings will then be cooked and will feel firm. Lift them out with a perforated spoon and drain in a sieve or strainer. The dumplings can also be made a day ahead of time, then warmed again in the soup.

To assemble the soup, heat the beef consommé to boiling. Bring the meatballs and dumplings to room temperature. Scoop the consommé into eight individual soup dishes. Add 1 tablespoon carrots and 1 tablespoon peas to each bowl. Add 5 meatballs and 5 dumplings to each bowl. Garnish with chervil and serve immediately.

8 servings

SUGAR-BROWNED POTATOES

1½ pounds small, firm potatoes

3 tablespoons sugar

3 tablespoons butter

The Danes serve Sugar-browned Potatoes at every celebratory meal. Small, whole potatoes work best.

Wash the potatoes, place them in a deep pot, cover with water, and bring to a boil. Cook for 15 to 20 minutes, or just until tender. Remove the pot from the heat, pour off the water, and rinse the potatoes in cold water. When the potatoes have cooled enough to handle, peel off their skins and set aside.

In a heavy frying pan or skillet, over medium heat, melt the sugar. When the sugar turns light brown around the edges, add the butter and stir until melted.

Rinse the peeled potatoes in cold water. Drain the potatoes and add them to the caramelized butter-sugar mixture. Cook the potatoes, shaking the pan often, until the potatoes are evenly glazed and heated through, which will take about 10 minutes.

6 servings

Brunede Kartofler

Glaserte Poteter

Glassrod Potatis

Every cook has his or her own method of achieving the "best" crackling pork crust. Else Andersen, an established Danish cook and cookbook writer, roasts the pork with the fat side down, with water in the pan, for 20 minutes, and then turns it over to finish cooking. Although many use a fresh leg of pork (or ham), my recipe is based on a pork loin. Ask the butcher for a pork loin with the fat cover left on top, the backbone removed, and the ribs left in place.

1 pork loin, about 5 pounds

3 teaspoons coarse kosher-style salt

12 bay leaves

1 quart boiling water

Preheat oven to 450°F.
Score the loin using a sharp knife in ½-inch intervals lengthwise and about 2-inch intervals across. Make the cuts about ½-inch deep. Rub the rind with the salt. Insert bay leaves in the cuts.

Place the roast on a rack in a roasting pan. Roast for 30 minutes. Pour the boiling water into the roasting pan, reduce the heat to 350°F, and continue roasting until the meat reaches 160°F in the center (insert an instant-reading thermometer into the center of the thickest part of the flesh, being careful not to let the thermometer touch the bone or fat). It should take about 1 hour. If necessary, add more boiling water to the pan if all the water you put in boils away.

Remove the roast from oven and cut off the crackling while it is still warm. Place the crackling in a separate dish, uncovered. Serve warm or chilled. If it will be served chilled, you may prepare the roast a day ahead, cut off the ribs, and slice the meat thinly.

8 to 10 servings

Flaesksteg

SWEET-AND-SOUR RED CABBAGE

1 small head red cabbage, shredded

4 tart fresh apples, peeled and thinly
sliced

1 to 1½ cups port wine

½ cup red currant jelly

1½ teaspoons lemon juice

1 teaspoon salt

Cooked red cabbage is extremely popular in all of Scandinavia. It is served not only with everyday meats, such as juicy sausages or stewed pot roasts, but also with celebration dishes like roast pork with cracklings. It will stay fresh for about a week in the refrigerator, and actually tastes best a day after it is cooked. Reheat it to serve with hot roast pork, or serve chilled with cold roast pork.

In a large, heavy-bottomed pot, combine the cabbage, apples, wine, jelly, lemon juice, and salt. Bring to a boil, cover, and lower heat to simmer for 1½ hours, stirring occasionally. Add more port if the cabbage becomes dry. Season with salt and transfer to a serving dish.

6 to 8 servings

Rødkål

Punakaali

Rødkål

Rödkål

This frozen dessert has the texture and flavor of vanilla ice cream. Cut it into wedges and serve with ginger cookies on the side.

L ine a 9-inch springform or deep cake pan with plastic wrap. Place the egg whites in a large metal mixing bowl. Place the egg yolks in a medium-sized bowl. Keep ready a shallow pan of simmering water. Whip the egg whites until frothy, then slowly beat in ¼ cup of the sugar. Place the bowl of egg whites over the simmering water and beat them with a hand-held mixer set at high speed, gradually adding ¼ cup more of the sugar, until the mixture is glossy, thick, and fluffy. Remove the egg white mixture from the heat and set aside. Keep the water simmering. Beat the egg yolks until frothy, then gradually add the remaining ½ cup sugar. Place the egg yolk mixture over the simmering water and beat at high speed until thick and frothy. Remove from the heat. Beat the cream cheese into the egg yolk mixture until light. Beat in the lemon rind and vanilla. Fold the yolk mixture into the whites.

In a separate bowl, beat the cream until thick. Fold into the egg mixture. Turn the batter into the prepared pan, cover it tightly, and freeze for 4 to 8 hours or longer. To serve, remove from the freezer 15 minutes before serving and cut into wedges. Top with lingonberries.

8 servings

ICE CREAM CAKE

3 eggs, separated

1 cup sugar

2 (8-ounce) packages cream cheese, at room temperature

Grated rind of 1 lemon

1 teaspoon vanilla extract

1½ cups heavy (whipping) cream

Lingonberries, for garnish

Iskage

Jäätelökakku

SCANDINAVIAN MEATBALLS

MASHED POTATOES

CHRISTMAS SEASON LUTEFISK AND MEATBALL DINNER

Although it wasn't originally just a holiday food, *lutefisk* has come to be associated with the Christmas season, especially among Scandinavian Americans. In areas of America where there are substantial numbers of families with Scandinavian roots, *lutefisk* and meatball dinners are a regular pre-holiday community event, and many hosts and hostesses serve it on Christmas Eve. It is available during the Christmas season in delicatessens and meat and fish markets wherever Scandinavians are found. ■ *Lutefisk*, because of its distinctive aroma, texture, and traditional method of curing with lye, is the butt of quite a few jokes. It is made of ling, a variety of codfish, processed by an ancient method of lye-curing and drying. The curing process stems from the days when salt was a costly ingredient and lye was simple to make using wood ashes. The board-like dried fish has to be soaked for several days in several changes of fresh water before it is ready to cook, but the *lutefisk* that you buy today has already been soaked and is ready to be cooked. Depending on family tradition, the fish is served with either a cream sauce or a melted butter sauce. ■ Those who love *lutefisk,* love it. Those who don't are offered meatballs—another famous traditional Scandinavian food—as a substitute. Both are served with fluffy mashed potatoes, a mainstay and an art in Scandinavia.

MENU

SCANDINAVIAN MEATBALLS
AND GRAVY

MASHED POTATOES

OVEN-STEAMED LUTEFISK WITH
BUTTER SAUCE OR CREAM SAUCE

BUTTERED GREEN BEANS OR PEAS

APPLE, BEET, AND RED
CABBAGE SALAD

CHRISTMAS RICE PUDDING WITH
CRANBERRY RASPBERRY SAUCE

SCANDINAVIAN MEATBALLS AND GRAVY

5 to 6 tablespoons butter

1 tablespoon minced onion

⅔ cup soft bread crumbs

1 cup water

¾ pound lean ground beef

¼ pound lean ground pork

1 teaspoon salt

½ teaspoon ground allspice

½ teaspoon ground white pepper

½ teaspoon sugar

2 tablespoons flour

2 cups beef broth

This basic, generations-old, authentic recipe has as many variations as there are cooks. Such recipes are found in the family cookbook and are usually called "Mother's Meatballs." What makes Scandinavian meatballs different from others is that the ground meat is beaten until it is light and fluffy. The resulting meatballs have a very light texture.

Melt 1 tablespoon of the butter in a large skillet. Add the onion and sauté for 1 to 2 minutes, until tender. In a large bowl of an electric mixer, combine the bread crumbs and water and let stand 1 to 2 minutes. Add the beef, pork, salt, allspice, white pepper, and sugar. Beat on low speed until smooth. Turn the mixer to high speed and beat until the meat mixture is light and fluffy, about 10 minutes. (Meat will lighten in color during beating.) Dip 2 teaspoons in ice water. Using the spoons, shape the meat into tiny meatballs (they may be slightly oval shape). Melt the remaining butter in a frying pan and place over medium heat. Add the meatballs and brown on all sides, constantly shaking the pan so they brown evenly on all sides. Drain the meatballs on paper towels, then transfer to a serving platter and cover to keep warm. When all the meatballs are cooked, add the flour to the skillet and stir over medium heat until the flour is lightly browned. Slowly add the beef broth and cook, stirring, until gravy is thick and brown. Strain if desired. Pour the gravy over the meatballs and serve hot.

6 servings

Svensk Frikadeller

Lihapyörykät

Kjøttkaker

Köttbullar

MASHED POTATOES

The art of making perfect mashed potatoes is one that every Scandinavian cook learns. First, select smooth, firm potatoes with a dry, mealy texture, such as Russets or all-purpose potatoes, both of which have rather thick skin. Once cooked, mash and then beat them with a potato masher or an electric mixer, until all the lumps are gone. Always add hot rather than cold milk to prevent the potatoes from getting glutinous and cold. Scandinavians like their mashed potatoes with an "eye" of both butter and gravy.

Pare, quarter, and rinse the potatoes. Place into a pot and cover with water. Add the salt to the water. Heat to boiling and cook for 20 to 30 minutes, until the potatoes are tender but not mushy. Drain. With an electric mixer, or potato masher, mash and beat the potatoes until smooth and fluffy. Slowly add the milk and butter, and beat again until smooth and fluffy. Season with salt, if desired. Serve immediately.

4 to 6 servings

3 pounds thick-skinned potatoes, such as Russets or all-purpose

2 teaspoons salt

¼ cup hot milk

3 tablespoons butter

Kortoffelmase

Perunavoi

Potetmose

Potatismos

OVEN-STEAMED LUTEFISK

3 pounds ready-to-cook lutefisk

1 tablespoon butter

2 teaspoons salt

CREAM SAUCE

3 tablespoons butter

2 tablespoons flour

2½ cups light cream or milk

½ to 1 teaspoon salt

⅛ teaspoon white pepper

1 egg yolk

BUTTER SAUCE

1 cup (2 sticks) butter

⅓ cup hot water

3 tablespoons lemon juice

Preheat oven to 350°F. Generously butter a baking dish, preferably one with a cover.

Place the fish, skin-side down, in the baking dish. Dot with the butter and sprinkle with the salt. Cover. (Use aluminum foil if your baking dish does not have a cover, but be sure that the foil does not touch the fish.)

Bake for 35 to 45 minutes, or until the fish flakes. (It may have a gelatinous appearance even though it is cooked.)

To make the cream sauce, in a heavy saucepan, melt the butter. Stir in the flour until well blended. Over medium heat, stir in the cream (or milk) and cook, stirring, until thickened. Add the salt and pepper. In a small bowl, add a little of the sauce to the egg yolk and mix well. Return the yolk mixture to the sauce and cook for 1 minute longer.

To make the butter sauce, in a saucepan, melt the butter. Stir in the hot water and lemon juice. Serve in a gravy boat with a spoon or ladle so it can be stirred with each serving.

Serve the fish hot with cream sauce or butter sauce.

6 servings

Paistettu lipeäkala

Kokt lutefisk

Ungskokt lutfisk

SCANDINAVIAN FEASTS

OVEN-STEAMED LUTEFISK WITH CREAM SAUCE

APPLE, BEET, AND RED CABBAGE SALAD

2 large apples, cored, unpared, chopped

1½ cups finely chopped pickled beets

3 to 6 cups finely shredded red cabbage

2 to 3 tablespoons lemon juice

Pinch of sugar and salt

Simple and fresh-tasting, you'll find this salad, or a very similar one, on every Swedish Christmas table. Combinations of red cabbage, beets, and apples, or sometimes just red cabbage alone, are very popular salads throughout Scandinavia. The dressing is simply lemon juice with sugar and salt, to taste.

In a bowl, combine the apples, beets, and cabbage. Sprinkle the lemon juice over the combination and add the sugar and salt. Toss to blend. Serve chilled.

6 to 8 servings

Rødkålsalat

Punakaalisalaatti

Rødkålsalat

Röd Julsallad

This rice pudding, which is flavored with cardamom, has a more custardy consistency than most rice puddings. Some people eat it plain, others like to top it with cinnamon sugar and cream. Finns like to pour a thickened fruit juice sauce over each serving. Whoever finds the almond in his or her pudding is given a special treat.

You can use any red fruit juice to make the sauce, but I like to use a cranberry-raspberry combination, which is available commercially.

Bring 1½ cups water to a boil. Add the rice and salt. Cover and simmer over low heat for 10 to 15 minutes, until the rice has absorbed the water.

Preheat oven to 325°F. Butter a deep 2-quart casserole dish.

Add the cream, milk, eggs, butter, sugar, and cardamom to the rice. Turn the mixture into the prepared casserole. Poke the cinnamon stick into the rice and hide the almond in the pudding.

Set the casserole into a larger pan and pour boiling water into the larger pan so that it reaches halfway up the edge of the casserole.

Bake for 2 hours, or until the rice swells and has a creamy texture.

To prepare the sauce, about 15 minutes before you are ready to serve the pudding, in a saucepan, combine the cranberry-raspberry and lemon juices with the cornstarch. Heat to boiling and simmer, stirring, until thickened and clear. Taste and add sugar if desired. Stir until sugar is dissolved. Cover and partially cool.

Serve the rice pudding warm or cooled, with the warm sauce poured over it.

6 to 10 servings

¾ cup uncooked short- or medium-grain rice

½ teaspoon salt

2 cups heavy (whipping) cream

2 cups milk

2 eggs, beaten

1 tablespoon butter

⅓ cup sugar

½ teaspoon freshly ground cardamom

1 (3-inch) stick cinnamon

1 whole almond

CRANBERRY RASPBERRY SAUCE

4 cups bottled cranberry-raspberry juice

1 tablespoon lemon juice

2 tablespoons potato starch or cornstarch

Sugar to taste

Risengrød
Riisipuuro
Risrynsgrøt
Julgröt

SAINT MARTIN'S DAY FEAST OF THE GOOSE

n Denmark and in the Swedish province of Skåne, it is traditional to have a goose dinner on the eve of St. Martin's Day, November 10th. According to one story, the date was originally celebrated in honor of a monk named Martin who was killed on that day. Another story says that Martin was so beloved by the people that they wanted him to become their bishop, but Martin, preferring to remain a monk, hid from them in a flock of geese. The cackling of the geese led his followers to his hiding place, and as an act of revenge, Martin killed a

goose and cooked it for dinner. ■ When Lutheranism gained popularity in Sweden, the feast began to be held in honor of Martin Luther. The traditional Swedish menu begins with *svartsoppa,* or Black Soup, made with the blood of the goose. For this menu, I chose to include the Danish fruit soup called *Kråsesuppe,* which is prepared with fruit and the giblets from the goose. One might embellish this menu with a simple red cabbage and apple salad (see page 154), which is frequently found on holiday and celebration tables along with Sugar-browned Potatoes.

MENU

DANISH FRUIT SOUP

ROAST GOOSE WITH APPLE AND
PRUNE STUFFING

SPICED PEARS

SUGAR-BROWNED POTATOES
(SEE PAGE 144)

SWEDISH BERRY PARFAIT

ROAST GOOSE

DANISH FRUIT SOUP

SOUP STOCK

6 cups water

1 medium-sized carrot, coarsely
   chopped

1 leek, coarsely chopped

½ cup diced celery root

3 sprigs parsley

2 teaspoons salt

1 bay leaf

2 whole cloves

Giblets from one goose, washed

SOUP

1 cup pitted prunes, chopped

3 medium apples, pared, cored, and
   chopped

1 cup water

1 tablespoon butter

2 tablespoons flour

1 egg yolk

⅓ cup heavy (whipping) cream

½ teaspoon salt

1 teaspoon vinegar

Dash of pepper

2 tablespoons dry sherry

Kråsesuppe

The Danes enjoy this soup with their autumn goose dinner and also as a first course during the Christmas season, followed by *aebleskiver,* or Danish pancakes.

Combine all of the stock ingredients in a 3-quart pot. Heat to simmering, cover, and simmer for 2 to 3 hours, until the giblets are tender, periodically skimming off any foam that forms. Strain the stock, discarding all but the giblets and the stock. Chop the giblets and return them to the stock. Cover the stock and continue to simmer.

While the stock simmers, in a saucepan, combine the prunes, apples, and water. Simmer for 20 minutes, or just until the prunes and apples are tender and have absorbed most of the water.

In a large soup pot, melt the butter. Add the flour and stir over medium heat for about 2 minutes, until lightly browned. Gradually stir in the stock and simmer for 5 minutes. In a small bowl, beat together the egg yolk and cream, just until blended. Add a small amount of the hot broth, stirring vigorously. Return the mixture to the soup, stirring. Add the prunes and apples. Season with salt, vinegar, pepper, and sherry. Serve hot.

6 servings

ROAST GOOSE WITH APPLE AND PRUNE STUFFING

Preheat oven to 325°F.

Wash the goose and dry with paper towels. Rub inside and out with the lemon, salt, and pepper.

Stuff the goose with the apples and prunes and close the large opening with a skewer. Close the small opening by overlapping the neck skin and back and securing with skewers. Loop string around the legs and tighten slightly. Place on a rack in a roasting pan, breast-side down.

Roast, uncovered, for 1 hour. Lift the goose out the pan and pour off and discard the fat from the pan. Return the goose to the pan so the breast side is facing up and pour the wine (or apple juice) over it. Roast until tender, for a total of about 25 minutes per pound, piercing the skin often to release the fat.

Place goose on a serving platter and keep warm.

To prepare the gravy, remove most of the fat from the pan. Strain the pan juices and pour the drippings into a saucepan. Mix together the cornstarch and water, then stir into the drippings. Simmer for 5 minutes, whisking constantly. Season with salt and pepper.

8 servings

10- to 12-pound goose

½ lemon

2 teaspoons salt

½ teaspoon pepper

5 apples, peeled, cored, and quartered

1 (12-ounce) package pitted prunes, about 2 cups (cooked according to package directions)

2 cups dry white wine or apple juice

1 tablespoon cornstarch

¼ cup water

Salt and pepper

Stegt gas med aebler og svesker

Paistettu hanhi

Stekt gas fylt med frukt

Fruktfylld stekt gås

SPICED PEARS

8 pounds small, firm pears (such as Little Seckels)

12 (3-inch) sticks cinnamon

2 tablespoons whole cloves

2 tablespoons whole allspice

2 cups water

1 quart white vinegar

8 cups sugar

In the old days in Scandinavia, fruit was a luxury reserved for special occasions. In this recipe, fresh pears are preserved so that they can be enjoyed later—with roasted poultry and ham during the holiday season, on a smorgasbord table, or on a breakfast buffet.

Wash the pears and remove the blossom ends. Place the pears in a large nonaluminum pot and cover them with water. Heat the water to boiling and boil for 10 minutes. Drain. With a fork, pierce the skins of each pear in 2 or 3 places.

Place the cinnamon, cloves, and allspice in a little bag made of a double thickness of cheesecloth and close securely with a piece of string.

In a 3- to 4-quart saucepan, combine the water, vinegar, sugar, and spice bag. Bring the mixture to a boil and boil for 5 minutes, until the mixture is syrupy. Remove the pan from the heat and place the pears in the syrup. Cover and set aside to cool overnight.

The next day, remove the spice bag and the pears and bring the syrup to a boil, stirring continuously to prevent scorching.

Pack the pears in eight sterilized pint jars and pour the hot syrup over them. Top with sterilized lids and bands.

Process in a boiling water bath for 20 minutes. Remove from the bath and cool. Label and store.

8 pints

Syltede Paerer

Maustettu Päärynät

SWEDISH BERRY PARFAIT

I usually hoard jars of lingonberry and cloudberry preserves just so I can use them to make this dessert. But they are full of seeds, so need to be strained. If neither is available, I substitute raspberry jam or cranberry preserves. This dessert can be made ahead of time and taken out of the freezer before serving to soften slightly.

In the top of a double boiler, over simmering water, beat the eggs and sugar, until thick. Remove the egg-sugar mixture from the heat and beat until cool. In a large bowl, whip the cream until it forms soft peaks. Add the vanilla. Stir the whipped cream and preserves (or jam) into the egg mixture, then pour the batter into a 1½ quart loaf pan or ring mold. Place in the freezer for at least 4 hours.

To prepare the berry sauce, place the berries in a blender and process until smooth. Strain through a sieve to remove the seeds. Blend in the powdered sugar and lemon juice.

Remove the parfait from the freezer 15 to 20 minutes before serving. Just before serving, turn it out of the pan and cut into 8 portions. Garnish with the almonds and serve with the berry sauce.

8 servings

2 eggs

½ cup powdered sugar

1¼ cups heavy (whipping) cream

1 teaspoon vanilla extract

½ cup strained lingonberry or cloudberry preserves, or cranberry preserves or raspberry jam

BERRY SAUCE

2 cups fresh or frozen raspberries, strawberries, or blackberries

½ cup powdered sugar

1 tablespoon lemon juice

2 tablespoons sliced almonds, toasted, for garnish

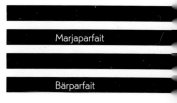

Marjaparfait

Bärparfait

GOOSÉBERRY PUDDING

ALMOND RUSKS

SUMMERTIME FRESHWATER SALMON FEAST

In central Sweden, in the beautiful province of Dalarna, the paintings of stylized naturalistic artists such as Carl Larsson and Anders Zorn come to life: the birch trees, lilac bushes, red houses with white trim, and scenes of company drinking coffee outdoors around picnic tables. ■ In the village of Tällberg there, the midsummer celebration, with music, folk dances, crafts demonstrations, boat races, swimming, and lots of good food, lasts all summer long. Many of the local clear freshwater lakes are used for fish farming, the preferred fish being freshwater salmon, which has a finer texture and a more delicate taste than ocean salmon, and cooks quickly. On

MENU

FRESH GARDEN LETTUCES WITH
LEMON AND SUGAR

SMOKED REINDEER OR BEEF SPIRALS
WITH HORSERADISH SAUCE

POACHED FRESHWATER SALMON

CUCUMBER SALAD

BOILED PARSLIED NEW POTATOES
AND PEAS

GOOSEBERRY PUDDING WITH CREAM

ALMOND RUSKS

◉◉◉◉

the shores of Lake Siljan, at Klockargården, one of Tällberg's charming inns, I enjoyed a memorable midsummer meal of cold, poached freshwater salmon and cucumber salad complemented by a bowl of hot, boiled potatoes. For dessert, I chose a soft meringue, aptly named Angel Pie, that was served with raspberries on top. In this menu, I've offered instead a dessert of chilled gooseberry pudding served with cream. The almond rusks are great cookies to keep on hand, especially during the summer when you don't want to heat up the oven. And the Smoked Reindeer or Beef Spirals are ideal when you need a pretty, make-ahead appetizer for a party.

FRESH GARDEN LETTUCES WITH LEMON AND SUGAR

1 quart fresh lettuces, washed and dried

¼ to ½ cup loosely packed fresh herbs, such as marjoram, chervil, cilantro, basil, or parsley

1 to 2 teaspoons sugar

1 to 2 teaspoons freshly squeezed lemon juice

Salt and pepper (optional)

It is the adventurous gourmets of Scandinavia who go to the trouble of growing variety lettuces, such as arugula and lamb's ears. The more typical gardener plants leaf lettuce, curly leaf lettuce, spinach, and maybe even a variety of herbs.

Arrange the lettuces on four individual salad plates, or toss in a salad bowl. Snip fresh herbs over the lettuces. Sprinkle with the sugar and lemon juice. Season with salt and pepper, if desired. Serve immediately.

4 servings

Salat

Salaatti

Salat

Sallad

Thinly sliced, smoked, and salted leg of reindeer is very similar in texture and character to Italian prosciutto. It isn't easy to find in the United States, although it is exported from Sweden and Finland. It makes a beautiful hors d'oeuvre on top of rye bread. Served as described here with horseradish sauce, it also makes an elegant first course. If reindeer meat is not available, you can substitute shaved roasted beef for a similar effect.

To prepare the sauce, fold the horseradish into the whipped cream. Add the lemon juice (or vinegar) and salt. Let the sauce stand for about 30 minutes to allow flavors to blend, or store in the refrigerator until ready to use.

To prepare the meat spirals, separate the slices of meat and lay flat. Combine the mustard and sour cream and spread on the meat. Twirl or twist the meat into spirals, then fan out one end to resemble the petals of a rose.

Arrange the meat on fresh butter lettuce leaves on individual salad plates or on a large platter. Serve with horseradish sauce.

4 servings

HORSERADISH SAUCE

½ cup freshly grated horseradish

½ cup heavy (whipping) cream, whipped

1 teaspoon fresh lemon juice or vinegar

½ teaspoon salt

MEAT SPIRALS

4 ounces thinly shaved smoked leg of reindeer or shaved beef

3 to 4 tablespoons strong mustard

¼ cup sour cream

Fresh butter lettuce leaves

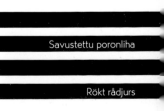

Savustettu poronliha

Rökt rådjurs

POACHED FRESHWATER SALMON

Fresh dill

6 (1-pound) whole freshwater salmon or trout, or 3 pounds fish fillets (each fillet should not exceed ½ pound in weight or 1 inch in thickness)

1 cup dry white wine or clam, fish, or chicken broth

1 tablespoon lemon juice

1 teaspoon salt

1 cup sour cream

Dill sprigs and lemon wedges, for garnish

The chinook salmon that is raised in the vacated iron pits of Northern Minnesota is almost identical to the salmon I ate in Tällberg, Sweden. You can, however, substitute almost any fish fillet that weighs half a pound or less.

Preheat oven to 400°F. Line a shallow 9-by-13-inch baking dish with fresh dill. Place the fish, side by side, on top of the dill. Pour the wine (or broth) over the fish and sprinkle with the lemon juice and salt. Cover tightly with foil. (You can do this step one day ahead of time and refrigerate.)

Bake the fish for 20 to 22 minutes, or until the fish flakes easily when probed with a fork. Let cool slightly, then pull off the skin. Strain the juices and boil them down until reduced to ½ cup. Mix in the sour cream.

To serve chilled, cover and refrigerate the fish for 2 hours or until ready to serve. Chill the sour cream sauce before serving.

To serve hot, arrange the fish fillets on a warm platter and serve with the warm sour cream sauce.

Garnish the fish with additional dill sprigs and lemon wedges.

6 servings

Kogt Laks

Keitetty Kirjolohi

Kokt Laks

Inkokt Lax

POACHED FRESHWATER SALMON

GOOSEBERRY PUDDING WITH CREAM

1 quart slightly unripe gooseberries, or 1 pound frozen gooseberries, or 2 cans whole gooseberries

1½ cups water (eliminate if using canned berries)

1 cup sugar (reduce to ½ cup if using canned berries)

2 tablespoons potato starch or cornstarch

Cold heavy (whipping) cream

Chilled thick puddings of this sort are ever so popular in Scandinavia. The pudding has to be thick so that you can swirl the cream on top.

Trim and rinse the fresh gooseberries. (If using canned berries, drain off the juice, measure it, and add enough water to measure 1½ cups.) Mix together the sugar and potato starch (or cornstarch).

Heat the water to boiling, add the fresh gooseberries, and simmer for 5 minutes. (If using canned berries, heat the juice-water mixture to boiling, add the gooseberries, and bring to a boil again.) Whisk in the sugar-and-starch mixture and cook, stirring constantly, until the pudding is thickened. Turn the pudding into a bowl, cover, and chill.

Spoon into serving dishes. Swirl the cream on the top of each serving.

6 servings

Stikkelsbaergrød

Karviaismarjakiisseli

Stikkelsebaergrøt

Krusbärskräm

ALMOND RUSKS

These twice-baked sweet rusks are perfect accompaniments to fruit desserts and ice creams. They will keep well in an airtight tin or jar.

Preheat oven to 350°F. Lightly butter or cover a baking sheet with parchment paper.

In a large mixing bowl, combine the egg and sugar and beat until thick. Add the butter, almonds, and almond extract. In a small bowl, mix the flour and baking powder, then stir into the wet ingredients.

Divide the dough into two parts. On a lightly floured board, roll out each part to make logs that are 1½ inches thick and 16 inches long. Place the logs on the prepared baking sheet. Bake for 20 minutes, or until firm. Reduce the oven temperature to 250°F. Cut the baked logs into ½-inch slices. Place the slices, cut-side up, on the baking sheet. Bake for 20 minutes longer. Turn the oven off but leave the rusks inside for another 20 minutes, or until crispy.

64 rusks

1 egg

½ cup sugar

½ cup (1 stick) butter, melted

½ cup unblanched almonds, chopped

½ teaspoon almond extract

1¼ cups flour

1 teaspoon baking powder

Mandelbrød

Mantelikorput

Mandelstenger

Mandelskorpor

DILL-COOKED CRAYFISH

FEAST OF THE CRAYFISH

Crayfish are nocturnal, and are caught at night in traps made of chickenwire. Attracted by the bait (usually a small fish), they swim into the trap through small funnel-shaped openings on each end and are unable to swim out. ■ Swedes and Finns vie in their reputation for crayfish feasts. Many have heard about the Swedish passion for crayfish, but for the Finns, eating crayfish is not only a passion, but a sport. For the better you are at cracking open the little crustaceans and sucking the meat, the more you get, all sportingly washed down with more vodka and more beer. ■ Eating crayfish is a ritual in itself, and after awhile, everyone develops his or her own style. Having logged my fair share of hours of practice, I recommend removing the pincers first, opening them with a knife, and then eating their meat by sucking it right out of the shells. Then, I lift the crayfish, turn it upside down, and pour the few drops of fluid right into my mouth. Or, you can pour them onto a piece of bread. Last and best is the meat in the tail. Remove the shell by cutting it along the side, turning it upwards; then remove the teaspoon-sized piece of meat and either eat it as is, or with a piece of bread. Some like to dip this small meaty tail, which is like a miniature lobster tail, in melted butter.

MENU

DILL-COOKED CRAYFISH

THINLY SLICED BREADS AND BUTTER

CHILLED VODKA OR AQUAVIT

BEER

MINERAL WATER

BLUEBERRY CHEESECAKE

◎◎◎◎

DILL-COOKED CRAYFISH

2 pounds uncooked crayfish (live or frozen and defrosted)

3 quarts water

⅓ cup salt

⅓ cup sugar

Large bunch fresh dill, preferably with crowns

Melted butter

Lemon wedges, for garnish

This is the simplest and best method for cooking fresh crayfish. It works well for shrimp and rock shrimp, too.

If using live crayfish, check to be sure they are all alive and discard any crayfish no longer alive. Rinse the crayfish in cold water. In a very large pot, combine the water, salt, sugar, and dill, reserving enough dill for the garnish. Bring to a boil.

Drop in the crayfish and bring to a boil again. Boil for 12 minutes. Drain the crayfish and allow them to cool. Refrigerate until ready to serve or mound on a tray and serve immediately garnished with more fresh dill. Serve with the melted butter and lemon wedges.

4 servings

Keitetty Ravut

Kräftor

August is the prime season for fresh blueberries, and this is one of the best ways to serve them—atop a mild lemon cheesecake.

Preheat oven to 400°F. Lightly butter a 9-inch round cake or tart pan with removable sides, or a springform pan.

To make the crust, in a large mixing bowl, combine the flour, baking powder, and sugar. Cut in the butter until the mixture resembles coarse crumbs. Blend in the egg yolk until the mixture makes moist crumbs. Press three-fourths of the mixture into the bottom and up 1 inch of the sides of the prepared pan. Bake for 15 minutes or just until lightly browned.

While the crust bakes, in a medium-sized bowl, cream the ricotta, cream cheese, lemon juice, lemon peel, vanilla, sugar, and eggs, until well blended. Pour the mixture into the baked crust. Reduce the oven temperature to 350°F and bake for 40 to 45 minutes, or until the filling is just set and the top is lightly browned. Top with the blueberries and the remaining crust batter. Bake for another 10 to 15 minutes, until lightly browned.

Remove from the oven and cool on a wire rack. Remove from the pan and serve with whipped cream, if desired.

8 servings

BLUEBERRY CHEESECAKE

CRUST

1 cup flour

1 teaspoon baking powder

2 tablespoons sugar

½ cup (1 stick) butter

1 egg yolk

FILLING

1 cup ricotta cheese

1 (8-ounce) package cream cheese

1 tablespoon lemon juice

2 teaspoons grated lemon peel

2 teaspoons vanilla extract

¼ cup sugar

2 eggs

1 pint fresh blueberries, washed and dried

¼ cup firmly packed brown sugar

1 cup heavy (whipping) cream, whipped (optional)

Mustikkapiirakka

GUDRUN'S RECIPE

In 1396, Queen Margrethe of Denmark declared that there must be a *kro* (or inn) every four Danish miles along the road. One Danish mile was equal to almost five American miles. This decree was changed in 1500, reducing the distance between inns to between two and three Danish miles, in order to accommodate the increasing number of travelers who were on foot or horseback. As a result of this tradition, Denmark today has many wonderful inns where guests can stay overnight and enjoy regional foods and special menus, along with the personal histories of the people of the area. ■ The Hvidsten Kro near the village of Hlad in Jutland dates back to 1634. It is one of the few oldest inns that was not destroyed either by fire or World War II. It was here that I heard about the "Recipe," which appears on menus throughout Denmark. It seems that when the country was pulling itself together after the Second World War, the "Recipe" was written by a Danish doctor as an example of what one should eat every day to stay healthy. Gudrun's Recipe, modeled after the doctor's plan, is the specialty of the house at the Hvidsten Kro. Gudrun was the proprietoress of the *kro* after the war and one of the first to put the idea of the "Recipe" into practice. It is imposing, as you can see. ■ On the menu also is a scaled down version of the "Recipe" called the "Half Recipe": sweet-and-sour fried herring; bread and butter; cheese; smoked fish; sliced cold cuts; liver pâté; bacon and egg cake with tomatoes, onions, and lettuce; and fresh berries. Even cut in half, Gudrun's Recipe is still an impressive meal. ■ Everything except the bacon and egg cake, a kind of country omelette, is made ahead of time and served cold. Danish restaurants offer the traditional recipe on midday menus and it is a great feast for an entertaining buffet.

MENU

BREAD AND BUTTER

CHEESE

CURED SALMON OR LAKE TROUT

SPICED SAUSAGE

DANISH LIVER PATE

BACON AND EGG CAKE WITH
TOMATOES, ONIONS, AND LETTUCE

SWEET-AND-SOUR FRIED HERRING

BEEF TENDERLOIN WITH
HORSERADISH SAUCE

GREEN BEANS WITH HERB BUTTER

DANISH PORK AND
BROWNED CABBAGE

BERRY PUDDING WITH CREAM

BERRIES IN SEASON WITH
WHIPPED CREAM

BACON AND EGG CAKE

DANISH LIVER PATE

1 pound chicken, pork, or calves livers, rinsed, connective tissues removed

1¼ pounds fresh boneless pork shoulder (including fat), cubed

1 medium-sized onion

2 teaspoons salt

3 eggs

½ cup heavy (whipping) cream

¾ teaspoon freshly ground white pepper

½ teaspoon freshly ground allspice

¼ teaspoon ground cloves

Most Danish cooks use either pork or calves livers for their pâté, but I prefer to use chicken livers. This recipe is best made a day ahead of time and refrigerated.

In a food processor fitted with a steel blade, process the liver until liquefied. Press the liquid through a sieve to remove any remaining connective tissues. Add the remaining ingredients to the food processor, and process until smooth. Add the strained liver and process until blended.

Preheat oven to 300°F. Butter a 9-by-5-inch loaf pan. Turn the liver mixture into the loaf pan and place it in a larger pan. Pour enough water into the large pan to reach about 2 inches up the loaf pan. Bake in the oven for about 2 hours, or until set in the center.

Remove the loaf pan from the larger pan and place a weight on top of the pâté. (I use a brick wrapped in foil.) Allow the pâté to cool, weighted, in the loaf pan. Unmold onto serving dish when cool or chilled and ready to serve.

Approximately 2 pounds, or 20 thin slices

Leverpostej

Maksapasteija

Leverpostei

Leverpastej

At a traditional Danish lunch, this baked omelette is often served after a tray of cold herring, salmon, bread, and salads has been enjoyed.

In a heavy, broilerproof skillet, cook the bacon until crisp. Drain and set aside. In a medium-sized bowl, beat together the flour, milk, eggs, salt, and pepper, until blended. In the skillet, heat the butter just until it begins to brown. Pour in the egg mixture. Cook over medium-high heat, until the omelette sets on the bottom. If desired, set the skillet under the broiler to brown the top of the omelette. Arrange the bacon on top of the omelette. Cut the omelette into wedges and serve directly from the pan, garnished with the chives, parsley, tomato, onion, and lettuce.

2 to 4 servings

BACON AND EGG CAKE

½ pound thick bacon slices, preferably unsmoked

1 tablespoon flour

6 tablespoons milk

4 eggs

½ teaspoon salt

¼ teaspoon freshly ground white pepper

1 tablespoon butter

GARNISH

Chopped chives

Parsley

Tomato wedges

Sliced sweet onions

Butter lettuce

Aeggekage med Bacon

SWEET-AND-SOUR FRIED HERRING

12 fresh, boneless, skinned fillets of
  herring, or other small fish, such as
  walleye or pike

½ cup rye flour

1 teaspoon salt

½ teaspoon pepper

3 to 4 tablespoons butter

1 large, sweet onion (such as Vidalia),
  cut crosswise into slices

SAUCE

¾ cup white wine vinegar

⅓ cup water

4 tablespoons sugar

6 whole peppercorns

1 teaspoon mustard seeds

Fresh fish of any kind, as long as it is small and lean, is delicious prepared this way. It is wonderful served hot, with the sauce poured over it, and equally tasty served cold, having marinated in the sauce for a day. Sometimes the Danes put it on top of a slice of well-buttered black bread to make an open-faced sandwich or *smørrebrød*.

Wash the fish fillets and pat them dry. In a medium-sized bowl, mix together the flour, salt, and pepper. Dredge the fillets in the flour mixture. In a heavy skillet, melt the butter. Over medium-high heat, add the fillets and brown for about 1 minute on each side, until lightly browned. Arrange the fillets in a shallow dish in a single layer. Top with the onion.

To prepare the sauce, in a saucepan, combine the vinegar, water, sugar, peppercorns, and mustard seeds and bring to a boil immediately. Pour the boiling sauce over the fish and serve hot, at room temperature, or chilled.

6 servings

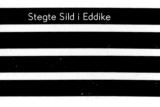

Stegte Sild i Eddike

In Denmark, Norway, and Sweden, cold fillet of beef is called "Roast-beef," and any other roast of beef is called *oksesteg*. The cold meat should be cut into very thin slices, placed on buttered rye bread, and garnished with remoulade, creamed horseradish, and/or mustard sauce.

Preheat oven to 375°F. Cut a piece of heavy-duty aluminum foil large enough to wrap around the roast. Spread the butter to within 3 inches of the edges of the foil. Press the garlic, pepper, and salt onto the surface of the roast. Place the meat on the center of the buttered foil. Close the foil securely using a drug-store wrap (align the long edges of the foil together above the roast and fold them down to form a lengthwise seam on top of the roast, then fold in the ends of the foil against the roast to form an airtight packet). Place the foil-wrapped roast on a rack in a roasting pan. Roast for 30 minutes for rare or 40 minutes until medium rare. Remove from the oven, adjust the oven rack to the top level, and turn on the broiler. Unwrap the foil and pull it back away from the meat, and broil just until the meat is browned, turning the meat once, for about 10 minutes in all. Remove the roast from the pan and wrap the foil around the meat again. Place the roast in a shallow dish, cover, and chill for at least 2 hours or overnight. To serve, cut into thin slices and serve with bread and horseradish (or other) sauce.

6 to 8 servings

2 pounds trimmed beef tenderloin

3 tablespoons butter, at room temperature

2 cloves garlic, finely minced (not crushed or pressed)

1 teaspoon coarsely cracked black peppercorns

1 teaspoon coarse salt

Horseradish sauce (see page 165)

Roastbeef i peberrod

Piparjuuripihvi

Roastbeef med pepperrotsaus

Pepparrots Roastbeef

DANISH PORK AND BROWNED CABBAGE

1 large head white cabbage

¼ cup sugar

¼ cup (½ stick) butter

2 pounds boneless pork back ribs or country-style ribs

Salt and pepper

When I was reminiscing about favorite "down home" foods with Bo Nielsen and Per Meyn, two chefs from Odense, this dish was described thus: Put sugar in a big pot. Melt it down. Add shredded cabbage and stir until it has browned. Then add meat, any kind, fresh or cured, and add water if you need to. Put the cover on and let it cook for 1½ hours. Serve the meat with mustard or mustard sauce, and rye bread. It sounded so satisfying, I could hardly wait to go home and try it.

Divide the cabbage into 8 portions and shred coarsely. Put the sugar in a large, preferably cast-iron, pot or Dutch oven, over low heat, and stir the sugar until it has melted and caramelized (but has not burned). Stir in the butter until blended. Add the cabbage, one handful at a time, browning each addition before adding the next. When all the cabbage has been browned, cover and steam for 45 minutes. Add the pork and bury the pieces within the cabbage. Cover and cook over low heat for 1 more hour.

Season with salt and pepper. Spoon the cabbage onto a platter. Top with the pork. Serve with mustard.

6 servings

Flaesk i Brunkaal

This delicious pudding is always made with red fruits or berries and is the traditional dessert after the classic Danish "Recipe." Potato starch is the preferred thickening agent in this and many other desserts because it produces clear juices of a consistency similar to corn syrup. It is available at Scandinavian specialty shops.

I n a large, heavy nonaluminum saucepan, blend the fruit juice, potato flour (or arrowroot or tapioca), and sugar to taste. Let stand for 15 minutes. Cook over medium heat, stirring constantly, until the mixture comes to a boil. Simmer until clear, stirring all the time. The pudding should be the consistency of corn syrup. Cover and cool. Pour the pudding into individual serving dishes or into a large glass bowl. Sprinkle the top with sugar and sliced almonds. Serve at room temperature or chilled. Serve with whipped cream.

6 to 8 servings

8 cups red fruit juice, such as
  strawberry, red currant, raspberry,
  blackcurrant, or cranberry, or a
  combination

½ cup potato starch or arrowroot or
  minute tapioca

Approximately 1 cup sugar

½ cup sliced almonds

Whipped cream, for serving

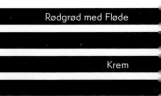

	Rødgrød med Fløde
	Krem

SWEDISH APPLE CAKE

SUPPERS

MIDNIGHT SUPPER ON THE WEST COAST OF SWEDEN

have to admit that when I first heard about a West Coast Salad from Swedish friends, I thought they were thinking about California. But obviously, its name comes from the west coast of Sweden. I later learned that this beautiful salad platter has long been a tradition in the early summer when days are long and the nights stay light, and it isn't uncommon to be invited to a midnight supper after a concert or the theater. When the sky is light throughout the night, it's a marvelous time for entertaining. ▪ Fish, shellfish, early summer vegetables, and sprigs of young dill are the basic components, but there are many variations depending on which west coast you are on, whether you are in Sweden or Norway—where both the salad and late-night entertaining are also popular in the summer—or even California. The shellfish may include a combination of mussels, oysters, shrimp, and lobster, or just one of them, depending on the catch and what you prefer. The vegetables can vary also, based on what you like and what is available.

MENU

WEST COAST SALAD

TOASTED FRENCH BREAD WITH
GREEN ONIONS AND DILL

CHOCOLATE MERINGUE DESSERT

SWEDISH APPLE CAKE

◎◎◎◎

In both Sweden and Norway, West Coast Salad is served as a main course at elegant post-theater suppers. It is typically made with shellfish caught along the Atlantic west coast, fresh vegetables, and a dill dressing. I like to arrange all of the components of the salad on a platter, but the Swedes quite often mix them all up in a bowl.

Heat a large pot of water to a boil. Add 1 tablespoon salt for each quart water. Add the shrimp (in their shells) and cook for 3 minutes, or just until pink. Remove from the pot, drain, cool, and refrigerate.

Heat the water to boiling again and add the lobster tails. Cook for 8 minutes, or just until pink. Remove from the pot, drain, cool, and refrigerate.

Pick over the crabmeat to remove any shells, and refrigerate.

If using mussels, scrub them and remove the beards. In a saucepan, heat the wine and shallot, until boiling. Add the mussels and cook for 2 minutes, uncovered, until the mussels open. Discard those that don't open. Drain and chill.

Cover a serving platter with crisp lettuce leaves. Shell and devein the shrimp. Arrange on the platter. Crack the lobster tails and remove the flesh. Cut the lobster into slices and arrange on the platter. Remove the mussels from their shells and arrange on top of the lettuce. Arrange the crabmeat in a pile. Arrange the mushrooms, asparagus, peas, tomatoes, and eggs in piles on the platter. Surround with thin wedges of lemon. Place the caviar on the platter. Garnish with fresh dill.

Continued on following page

WEST COAST SALAD

2 pounds medium-sized shrimp

2 lobster tails, about 1 pound each

1 pound fresh, cooked crabmeat

1 pound mussels (optional)

1 cup dry white wine (if using mussels)

1 shallot, chopped (if using mussels)

Iceberg or Romaine lettuce leaves

¾ pound small mushrooms, cleaned and quartered

1 pound fresh asparagus, trimmed, blanched, and chilled

1 cup fresh peas, or ½ pound snow pea pods, blanched and chilled

2 ripe tomatoes, peeled, seeded, and diced

3 hard-boiled eggs, cut into wedges

1 cup caviar

2 lemons, cut into wedges

Fresh dill, for garnish

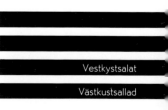

Vestkystsalat

Västkustsallad

Continued from preceding page

DILL DRESSING

½ cup salad oil

3 tablespoons white wine vinegar

6 tablespoons chopped fresh dill, or
  3 tablespoons dried dill weed

½ teaspoon salt

Dash of pepper

To prepare the dressing, in a small bowl, whisk together the oil, vinegar, dill, salt, and pepper. Just before serving, drizzle the dressing over the salad.

12 to 16 servings

CHOCOLATE MERINGUE DESSERT

¾ cup (about 6) egg whites

2 tablespoons cornstarch

1½ cups sugar

2½ cups heavy (whipping) cream

12 ounces semisweet or bittersweet
chocolate, chopped

1 cup slivered almonds, toasted

The literal translation of this dessert's name is "court" or "royal" dessert, and it is always appropriate for a festive occasion. But, do not try to make it on a hot and humid day. Whenever I have a few extra egg whites on hand, I whip up the meringues and freeze them in an airtight tin so that on the day of my next party, all I need to do is make the sauce, whip the cream, and build the pyramid.

Preheat oven to 250°F. Cover two baking sheets with parchment paper, or grease and heavily flour them.
In a large mixing bowl, beat the egg whites until frothy. In a separate bowl, mix the cornstarch and sugar, then add to the egg whites, beating at high speed until very stiff and glossy. Using a small ice cream scoop, shape the mixture into about sixty 1-inch balls. Place them 2 to 3 inches apart on the prepared baking sheets. Bake for 1 hour. Turn the oven off without opening the door and let the meringues dry in the cooling oven for at least 4 hours, or until the oven is cold.

In a small saucepan, combine ½ cup of the cream with the chocolate. Place over low heat and stir until the chocolate is melted and the sauce is smooth. Remove from the heat and cool.

Whip the remaining cream until it forms stiff peaks. Arrange one even layer of the meringues, covering the bottom of a large glass platter or shallow bowl. Spread with part of the cream. Arrange the remaining meringues into a pyramid-like structure, using the whipped cream as mortar to hold them together. Drizzle with the cooled chocolate sauce and sprinkle with the almonds. Serve immediately.

12 servings

Hofdessert

Hovijälkirouka

Hoffdessert

Hovdessert

SWEDISH APPLE CAKE

Scandinavians are masters at making wonderful desserts with apples. This is my version of a buttery, almond-topped cake that I enjoyed at a beautiful roadside coffee-stop in Sweden.

Preheat oven to 350°F. Butter a 10-inch springform pan or a 10-inch cast-iron skillet and sprinkle with the bread crumbs. In a large mixing bowl, beat the eggs and 1 cup of the sugar until thick and lemon-colored. Add the butter. In a separate bowl, combine the flour and baking powder, then add to the butter mixture. Pour the batter into the prepared pan (or skillet).

In a medium-sized bowl, combine the remaining ¼ cup sugar and the cinnamon. Toss the apples in the cinnamon-sugar mixture, until all the pieces are well coated. Press the apples into the top of the cake batter in a spiral pattern. Sprinkle with the almonds. Bake for 1 hour or until a skewer inserted in the center of the cake comes out clean. Serve hot or at room temperature.

12 servings

1 tablespoon fine dry bread crumbs

4 eggs

1¼ cups sugar

1 cup (2 sticks) butter, melted

1½ cups flour

1 teaspoon baking powder

2 teaspoons cinnamon

3 apples, pared and cut into 12 wedges

⅓ cup slivered or sliced almonds

Aeblekage

Omenakakku

Eplekake

Appelkaka

LOIN OF PORK WITH PRUNES

SWEDISH BROWN BEANS

FAT TUESDAY SUPPER

at Tuesday, also known as Shrove Tuesday, falls on the day before Ash Wednesday, which marks the beginning of Lent. In the past, this was the day when people consumed all kinds of rich foods to tide them over during the lean days of Lent, when dietary regulations and fasting were strictly enforced. In various parts of Sweden, Fat Tuesday was also known as "seven-meals-a-day," "pork day," and "butter day." Today, the strict rules and regulations of Lent have all but disappeared, but people still observe the season by eating traditional foods, beginning with buckwheat *blini* served with caviar, sour cream, chopped onion, and freshly ground allspice, and ending with *semlor,* or Fat Tuesday Buns—amazing yeast buns filled with whipped cream and marzipan and dusted with powdered sugar. Though traditional, I find Fat Tuesday Buns to be too rich to accompany this rather heavy supper. Instead, with this menu I usually substitute fresh fruit for dessert and save the Fat Tuesday Buns to serve for breakfast or brunch with a pot of good strong coffee and a pitcher of fresh fruit juice.

MENU

BUCKWHEAT BLINI

ICED SCHNAPPS AND CHILLED BEER
OR CHAMPAGNE

LOIN OF PORK WITH PRUNES

SWEDISH BROWN BEANS

FAT TUESDAY BUNS

◎◎◎◎

BUCKWHEAT BLINI

1 package active dry yeast

1¼ cups warm water (105°F to 115°F)

1 cup all-purpose flour

½ cup buckwheat flour

1¼ cups boiling milk

2 teaspoons salt

2 eggs, separated

1 tablespoon butter, melted

ACCOMPANIMENTS

Melted butter

Sour cream

Finely chopped sweet onion

Fresh whitefish, burbot, or salmon roe

Salt and pepper

Whole allspice, or white pepper, in a
    pepper grinder

These traditional buckwheat pancakes, or *blini,* are yeast-soured and raised. The batter is mixed up the night before they are to be cooked and is allowed to stand overnight and all day to sour. They are best served hot from the pan. Although some Finnish hostesses like to mix the sour cream and onion toppings together, and others will mix the fresh fish roe with whipped cream, I like to serve all the accompaniments separately so that guests can choose their own. As well as a first course, *blini* make a great late night snack, a fine light supper, and can also be served for breakfast or brunch, accompanied by sour cream, berries, fruit, or jam.

Buckwheat flour, which is available in most health food stores, should be stored in an air-tight container in the refrigerator.

In a large bowl, dissolve the yeast in the warm water. Stir in the all-purpose and buckwheat flours. Cover and let rise at room temperature for 8 to 24 hours. Once or twice during the rising period, uncover and beat the mixture with a spoon.

When ready to cook, stir in the boiling milk, salt, egg yolks, and melted butter. In a separate bowl, whisk the egg whites until stiff, then fold into the milk mixture.

To cook, spoon 2 tablespoons of batter into a buttered 6-inch crêpe pan and tilt the pan to spread the batter into a round. Bake until browned on one side, about 1½ minutes, then turn over and bake until browned on the other side, about 1 to 1½ minutes longer. The *blini* should be about ¼-inch thick and brown. Serve hot. Set out the accompaniments for guests to add as they wish.

4 to 6 servings

Linnit ja Madenmäti

BUCKWHEAT BLINI

LOIN OF PORK WITH PRUNES

3 pounds boneless loin of pork

12 to 14 pitted prunes, soaked in water
for 15 minutes

2 cooking apples, peeled, cored, and
sliced

1 tablespoon butter

1½ teaspoons salt

½ teaspoon freshly ground pepper

1 tablespoon potato starch or
cornstarch

For a Scandinavian-style Sunday feast, serve this stuffed pork loin with boiled potatoes, sautéed apple slices, cooked prunes, and currant jelly.

Preheat oven to 325°F.

With a long, thin-bladed knife, make a cut through the center of the pork loin. With the handle of a wooden spoon open up the hole. Stuff the hole with the prunes and apple slices, pressing them through to the center from each end of the roast.

Heat the butter in a heavy Dutch oven or roasting pan. Add the meat and brown on all sides. Sprinkle with the salt and pepper. Pour 2 cups water into the bottom of the pan. Roast in the preheated oven, uncovered, for one hour, or until the meat is done (when an instant-reading thermometer inserted into the center of the meat registers 160°F).

Remove the roast from the pan. Slice and arrange on a platter. Cover and keep warm. To make gravy, strain the juices in the pan and bring to a boil. Combine the potato starch (or cornstarch) with 1 tablespoon of water and whisk into the boiling juices, cooking until thickened.

6 to 8 servings

Fyldt Svinekam

Luumuilla silavoitu Sianselkäpaisti

Fylt Svinefilet

Plommonspäckad fläskkare

SWEDISH BROWN BEANS

If you cannot find Swedish brown beans, which are usually available in shops that specialize in Scandinavian foods, substitute pinto beans.

Rinse the beans and put them in a large pot. Cover with water and let stand overnight. Bring the water and the beans to a boil over medium-high heat, adding more water if necessary to cover the beans. Add the salt and crystallized ginger. Cover and simmer for 1½ hours or until the beans are tender. Using a potato masher, crush some of the beans. Add the vinegar, corn syrup, brown sugar, and ground ginger. Simmer for 30 minutes longer, or until thickened. Season with additional salt, vinegar, and corn syrup, if desired.

6 to 8 servings

2 cups Swedish brown beans or pinto beans

5 cups water

1 teaspoon salt

2 teaspoons crystallized ginger, chopped

¼ cup cider vinegar

¼ cup dark corn syrup

¼ cup firmly packed brown sugar

1 teaspoon ground ginger

Additional salt, vinegar, and corn syrup (optional)

Brune bønner

Ruskeat pavut

Brune bønner

Bruna bönor

FAT TUESDAY BUNS

1 package active dry yeast

¼ cup warm water (105°F to 115°F)

1 egg

⅔ cup milk, scalded and cooled

½ cup (1 stick) butter, softened

¼ cup sugar

½ teaspoon salt

½ teaspoon freshly ground cardamom

2¾ to 3 cups flour

1 beaten egg, for glaze

8 ounces almond paste, cut into
   16 pieces

½ cup heavy (whipping) cream,
   whipped

2 tablespoons powdered sugar

Additional powdered sugar, for dusting
   the buns

Hot milk, sugar, and cinnamon

Truthfully, I enjoy these almond-filled buns best in the morning for breakfast, with coffee and juice.

In a large bowl, dissolve the yeast in water. Let stand for 5 minutes. Beat in the egg, milk, butter, sugar, salt, and cardamom. Stir in 2 cups flour. Beat until smooth. Add enough of the remaining flour to make a stiff dough. Turn the dough out onto a lightly floured board, cover, and let rest for 15 minutes. Clean the bowl, then brush it lightly with vegetable oil. Knead the dough for 10 minutes, or until smooth and satiny. Place in the oiled bowl and turn over to coat. Cover with a cloth and let rise in a warm place until doubled, about 1 hour. Lightly grease or cover a large baking sheet with parchment paper. Preheat oven to 400°F.

Turn dough out onto a lightly oiled board. Divide the dough into four portions. Divide each portion into another four parts. Shape each piece of dough into a round bun, about 1-inch high and place on the baking sheet. Let rise until doubled, about 45 minutes. Brush with the beaten egg. Bake for 10 to 12 minutes, or until golden. Cool on rack.

About a third of the way down from the top of the bun, make a horizontal slit, leaving a "hinge" that keeps the top and bottom of the bun together. Open the bun and place a piece of almond paste and a spoonful of whipped cream inside. Dust with powered sugar.

To serve, place a bun in a deep dessert bowl that is about one-fourth filled with hot milk. Sprinkle with sugar and cinnamon. Eat with a fork and spoon. Unfilled buns can be frozen. Thaw and fill just before serving.

16 buns

Faşţelavnsboller

Laskiaispullat

Fastelavensboller

Semlor

FAT TUESDAY BUNS

Rømmegrøt, a rich, creamy pudding, is the "soul food" of Norway. It is served for all significant occasions, including Christmas, Midsummer's Day, Independence Day (May 17th), St. Olaf's Day (July 29th), anniversaries, birthdays, baptisms, weddings, and funerals. It is also prepared for special guests, new mothers, or as a gift for a hostess. Traditionally, it is transported in a wooden carrier on which the cook paints his or her own distinctive floral design, or *rosemaling*. ∎

One of the dangers, or pleasures, of being a visitor in Norway is being served lots of *rømmegrøt,* as it is also prepared for special guests. One day I was first served a delicious *rømmegrøt* by Arne Brimi, a bright

MENU

NORWEGIAN CELEBRATION CREAM PUDDING WITH CINNAMON AND SUGAR

EMBJORG'S CRISP FLATBREAD

CURED HAM OR REINDEER OR COLD ROAST BEEF

⊚⊚⊚⊚

young chef in Lom, who directed me to sprinkle it with cinnamon and sugar, and who served flatbread and shaved, cured reindeer meat as accompaniment. I next visited Embjorb Skamsar to learn how to make her special flatbread. She mixed, kneaded, and rolled out tissue-thin sheets of dough, flipping the rounds onto a wood-fired stove that baked them to thin, crisp perfection. She then served her superb flatbread with *rømmegrøt,* sprinkled with cinnamon and sugar, and shaved, cured reindeer meat. That evening, at dinner, I asked the innkeepers about the menu for their special Midsummer's celebration. What else? *Rømmegrøt* with cinnamon and sugar, flatbread, and shaved, cured reindeer meat.

In some parts of Norway, it is traditional for wedding guests to bring a large bowl of *rømmegrøt,* as a sort of "entry ticket" to the celebration. At the reception, the puddings are lined up for the guests to sample and to compare.

Although Norwegians consider *rømmegrøt* a main dish, this pudding makes a wonderful dessert when served with a sprinkling of cinnamon and sugar.

In a heavy-bottomed saucepan, bring the sour (or heavy) cream to a boil. Boil for 2 minutes, then add half the flour, whisking until it is well blended. Skim off and reserve the butter that is rendered out of the mixture. (The rendered butter will look like clarified butter.) Add the remaining flour, one tablespoon at a time. Stir in the milk. Simmer, whisking, for 5 to 6 minutes, until the pudding is very smooth. Cover and cool.

Serve with the reserved warm butter and cinnamon and sugar to sprinkle over the top.

6 to 8 servings

2 cups sour cream or heavy (whipping) cream

¾ cup flour

2 cups milk

Dash of salt

Cinnamon and sugar, for serving

Rømmegrøt

EMBJORG'S CRISP FLATBREAD

1 pound (about 3 or 4) medium-sized
    potatoes

1 cup buttermilk

1 cup whole milk

4 cups barley flour

1 to 1½ cups bread flour or unbleached
    all-purpose flour

Tvisteiktbrød

There are many types of flatbread and *lefse* in Norway. *Lefse* is a general term for a soft flatbread. Embjorg's flatbread is soft while warm, but crisp when cooled and eaten. Any flat-bottomed pancake griddle without sides works fine. A grooved flatbread or *lefse* rolling pin is ideal for the grooves make it easier to roll the dough out thinly, but a standard rolling pin will do. You will also need a bread board, and a weight for flattening the bread.

Put potatoes into a 2-quart pot and cover with water. Heat to boiling, reduce to a simmer, and cook for 25 to 30 minutes, or until the potatoes are tender, but the skins are not broken. Remove from the heat, pour off the water, and allow the potatoes to cool until you can handle them. Remove the potato skins. Press the potatoes through a ricer into a large mixing bowl or mash them using an electric mixer, but without adding any liquid.

Add the buttermilk, whole milk, and half the barley flour, stirring until the dough becomes stiff. Slowly add the remaining barley flour and half the bread (or unbleached all-purpose) flour. Turn out onto a lightly floured board and knead until the dough is smooth and well blended, adding more flour as necessary.

Divide the dough into four parts. Shape each part into a log and cut each into four parts to make 16 equal-sized pieces. Cut each piece in half to make 32 total.

Warm a pancake griddle with at least a 10-inch flat bottom over medium heat, until a drop of water bounces and sizzles on the surface.

Meanwhile, one portion at a time, roll dough out into a 10-inch round, adding flour as necessary. Using a spatula, carefully lift the round onto the dry, heated griddle. Grill for 1 to 2 minutes on each side, or until the side appears dry and has little brown spots on it. Fold in half right on the griddle and press out any air bubbles on the edges and at the fold. Fold again into quarters. Remove from the griddle and place on a bread board. Top with another board and place a weight on top (try canned goods or a brick). Repeat with the remaining portions of dough, keeping the rounds under the weights until all rounds are finished and the breads are cooled.

32 flatbreads

NORWEGIAN CELEBRATION CREAM PUDDING

EMBJORG'S CRISP FLATBREAD

AFTER-SKI SUPPER

In April, Sweden's southernmost country-side is brilliant with tulips, flowering lilacs, and apple blossoms. In Stockholm, the trees are leafing and the air is alive with springtime. But in Åre, in the northern foothills of the Caledonide Mountains, near the Norwegian border, Swedes are still skiing. In fact, there is a shush-boomer's race on the last day of every April that fills up all the local hotels, mountain huts, and camping sites with groups of families and friends. This mountainous region, called Jämtland, has always been a somewhat distinct province. The dialect spoken here seems to have more in common with Norwegian than Swedish, and in fact, Jämtland was part of Norway when Norway belonged to Denmark. ▪ After long days on the mountain—it is light until almost 10:00 P.M.—tired skiers relax over a bottle of Hummel, a beer produced by Åre's newly resurrected brewery, and wedges of Brie Pie or Swedish Onion Pie served with freshwater caviar and sour cream. Or, along with some flavorful, hot soup, they might choose the fresh white Swedish goat cheese—it resembles Greek feta—made at the nearby Husa cheese factory and marinated with herbs. For dessert I have included the ever-popular and delicious Almond Sugar Cake, romantically named after Puccini's *Tosca*—who could resist?

MENU

SWEDISH ONION PIE

GREEN KALE SOUP

BRIE PIE

HERB-MARINATED SWEDISH GOAT
CHEESE AND TOMATO SALAD

CUCUMBER AND FRESH
LETTUCE SALAD

ALMOND SUGAR CAKE

SWEDISH BEER AND SCHNAPPS

⊚⊚⊚⊚

SWEDISH ONION PIE

The flavor of onion and allspice combined is a popular one in Sweden. Wedges of this pie are topped with sour cream and golden *lojrom* (whitefish) caviar, which, in the United States, is sold in the freezer case in fish markets. Red salmon caviar can be substituted.

To prepare the pastry shell, put the flour and salt in a medium-sized bowl. Cut in the butter, until the mixture resembles coarse crumbs. Stir the lemon juice into 2 tablespoons of the ice water and sprinkle over the flour mixture, tossing until dough clings together. Add more water, if necessary. Shape into a ball and give it a couple of quick kneads on a floured surface. Cover with plastic wrap and chill for 30 minutes.

Preheat oven to 425°F. Roll the dough out into a 10-inch circle on a lightly floured board. Fit the pastry into a 9-inch fluted tart pan with a removable bottom, and press it into the bottom and sides of the pan. Line the pastry with waxed paper and fill with pie weights or beans.

Bake for 20 minutes, or just until the edges begin to brown. Remove the shell from the oven, cool slightly, and remove the weights.

To prepare the filling, preheat oven to 350°F. In a skillet, over low heat, sauté the sliced onions in the butter, until the onions are transparent (about 5 minutes). Remove from the heat and stir in the flour, eggs, half-and-half, salt, and allspice. Pour the egg mixture into the partially baked pastry shell. Sprinkle the shredded cheese over the top. Bake for 25 to 30 minutes, or until the pie is set in the middle.

Spread the sour cream on the top of the pie. Garnish each serving with a small spoonful of caviar.

12 appetizer wedges

BUTTER PASTRY SHELL

1 cup flour

¼ teaspoon salt

6 tablespoons (¾ stick) cold butter

2 teaspoons lemon juice

2 to 3 tablespoons ice water

FILLING

2 large onions, thinly sliced crosswise

5 tablespoons (¼ cup plus 1 tablespoon) butter

1 tablespoon flour

3 eggs

1 cup half-and-half

½ teaspoon salt

¼ teaspoon freshly ground allspice

1 cup shredded Adelost, Havarti, or a soft, mild white cheese

1 cup sour cream

¼ cup golden or red caviar, for garnish (optional)

Lökpaj

GREEN KALE SOUP

GREEN KALE SOUP

In old Sweden, this beautiful pale green soup was served as a symbol of hope and life on Maundy Thursday, a day on which evil spirits were believed to have been especially active. In some areas it is still traditional to make this soup every spring using seven different greens. Spinach works well instead of kale, and sorrel, young nettle leaves, or chard, alone or combined, will produce a delicious soup.

In a large pot, combine the greens, onions, and water. Heat to boiling and cook for 10 minutes, or until the onions are tender. Strain the liquid and return it to the pot. Transfer the greens to a food processor or blender and process until the leaves are chopped but not puréed, adding the flour while you are processing, pouring some of the cooking liquid into the processor, as needed, to keep the mixture fluid. Return the mixture to the pot with the cooking liquid and add the chicken broth. Heat to boiling and whisk in the salt, ginger, and white pepper. Stir in the cream. Garnish with the hard-boiled eggs and chives.

6 servings

1 pound fresh kale, spinach, young
    nettle leaves, sorrel, or chard,
    washed

6 green onions

2 cups water

2 tablespoons flour

2 cups chicken broth

1 teaspoon salt

⅛ teaspoon ground ginger

Freshly ground white pepper

½ cup light or heavy (whipping) cream

2 hard-boiled eggs, chopped

2 tablespoons chopped fresh chives

Grønkålsuppe

Lehtikaalisosekeitto

Grønnkålsuppe

Grönsuppa

BRIE PIE

1 small yellow bell pepper, seeded and sliced

1 small red bell pepper, seeded and sliced

2 tablespoons butter

1 partially baked 9-inch Butter Pastry Shell (see page 203)

¼ pound Brie cheese

3 eggs

1 cup heavy (whipping) cream

1 teaspoon salt

⅛ teaspoon white pepper

⅛ teaspoon nutmeg or mace

Thinly sliced gravlax, smoked meat, or ham, for garnish

Gherkins or olives, for garnish

Scandinavians are expert cheesemakers, and they use their cheeses in many classic dishes, such as this variation of quiche.

Preheat oven to 400°F.

In a skillet, over low heat, sauté the sliced bell peppers in the butter for 20 minutes, or just until tender. Turn the peppers into the partially baked pastry.

Cut the Brie into ½-inch wedges. Place on top of the bell peppers with one of the cut sides up, in a pinwheel fashion.

In a medium-sized bowl, beat the eggs, cream, salt, white pepper, and nutmeg (or mace), until well blended. Pour the egg mixture over the Brie and peppers in the pie shell.

Bake for 10 minutes, reduce the temperature to 350°F, and continue baking for about 30 minutes, or until the center of the pie is set. Cool for about 10 minutes before slicing. This can be served warm or cold. Garnish each slice with gravlax or meat that has been rolled into cornucopias, and pickles or olives.

12 appetizer servings

Briepaj

HERB-MARINATED SWEDISH GOAT CHEESE AND TOMATO SALAD

In the northwest part of Sweden, in the village of Husa, there is a small cheese factory that produces a white goat milk cheese, called Getost, that is similar to Greek feta. Marinated in a mixture of tomatoes, garlic, olive oil, vinegar, and herbs, it makes a welcome appetizer, salad, or first course.

C ut the cheese into ½-inch cubes. In a bowl, combine the cheese cubes, olive oil, vinegar, tomatoes, garlic, basil, oregano, chives, salt, and black pepper. Blend carefully with a rubber spatula. Serve immediately at room temperature on a bed of lettuce, or cover and store for up to 2 days in the marinade.

6 servings

½ **pound white Swedish goat cheese or Greek feta cheese**

¾ **cup olive oil**

¼ **cup white wine vinegar**

3 **medium cloves garlic, minced or crushed through a press**

2 **large, ripe tomatoes (about 1 pound), seeded and cubed**

2 **tablespoons minced fresh basil, or 1½ tablespoons dried**

1 **tablespoon minced fresh oregano, or 2 teaspoons dried**

1 **tablespoon minced fresh chives**

1 **teaspoon coarse salt**

Freshly ground black pepper

Fresh leaf lettuce, for garnish

Ortmarinerad Getost

ALMOND SUGAR CAKE

This classic butter cake is topped with a caramel and almond frosting that is broiled onto the cake after it is baked. The name for this cake, *Tosca,* is in the Scandinavian tradition of naming cakes after literary figures or operas.

Preheat oven to 350°F. Butter a 9-by-13-inch cake pan.

In a large mixing bowl, beat the eggs and sugar until light and lemon-colored. Fold in the melted butter. In a separate bowl, combine the flour and baking powder. Fold the dry ingredients into the egg mixture. Blend in the milk and vanilla. Pour the batter into the prepared pan and bake for 25 to 30 minutes, or until a toothpick inserted in the center comes out clean.

Meanwhile, to prepare the topping, in a saucepan, combine the butter, sugar, and cream. Cook over low heat, stirring constantly, until the mixture comes to a boil. Remove the cake from the oven and pour the topping over it immediately, smoothing it evenly. Sprinkle with the almonds.

Turn the broiler on and place the cake on the lowest rack away from the heat. Broil until the topping is bubbly and the almonds are lightly browned. Remove from the oven and cool. Cut into squares to serve.

12 servings

ALMOND SUGAR CAKE

4 eggs

1¼ cups sugar

¾ cup (1½ sticks) butter, melted and cooled

2 cups flour

2 teaspoons baking powder

¼ cup milk

1 teaspoon vanilla extract

ALMOND TOPPING

½ cup (1 stick) butter

½ cup sugar

½ cup heavy (whipping) cream

1 cup sliced or slivered almonds

Toscataerte

Toscakakku

Toscakake

Toscatårte

SALMON SOUP

SALMON SOUP SUPPER

When I was growing up I ate salmon soup often, but the most memorable bowlful I ever had was in a Helsinki restaurant several years ago on a hot summer day when I was homesick and hungry. Salmon soup is a standard item on Helsinki menus, and I ordered it with a sour rye bun and butter. The soup was perfect. Finnish potatoes have a creamy, rich flavor and the potatoes in my soup were cooked perfectly, just until they were tender but not mushy. The salmon was not at all overcooked but held its appealing color and shape; the leeks and celery offered separate and distinctive flavors that complemented each other beautifully. Even the bread and butter had an intense flavor. Why do I remember this meal so well? Partly, it is the remembrance of the wonderful flavors and the perfection of this simple preparation. But it could also be explained by the fact that it was a sure cure for what ailed me. The equally easy-to-prepare Blueberry Raspberry Pie that I've added to this menu provides a light and refreshing final touch.

MENU

SALMON SOUP

RYE BREAD

BLUEBERRY RASPBERRY PIE

SALMON SOUP

2 tablespoons butter

1 large onion, finely chopped

1 small leek, washed and finely sliced

1 stalk celery, finely sliced

2 tablespoons flour

3 cups water

1½ tablespoons lemon juice

12 ounces fresh salmon fillets, or cooked or smoked salmon

2 cups whole milk or light cream

¼ teaspoon freshly grated nutmeg

½ teaspoon ground ginger

Salt and white pepper

⅓ cup heavy (whipping) or light cream (optional)

½ cup chopped fresh dill, or 6 teaspoons dried dill weed, for garnish

Although I call for fresh salmon fillets in this recipe, you can use any salmon that is left over from another meal. Just be sure you don't overcook it. In a pinch, you can even use canned salmon.

Melt the butter in a heavy, 4-quart saucepan. Add the onion, leek, and celery and sauté over medium heat for 2 minutes, stirring constantly. Mix in the flour. Add the water and lemon juice and simmer, stirring occasionally, until lightly thickened. Cut the fish into thin slices if it is uncooked. Flake cooked or smoked fish. Add the fish and the milk (or light cream) to the pot and heat through but do not boil. Add the nutmeg and ginger. Season with salt and white pepper. Stir in the cream (optional). Ladle into soup plates and sprinkle with lots of fresh dill or dried dill weed.

6 servings

Lohikeitto

BLUEBERRY RASPBERRY PIE

Finnish cooks use a variety of pastries to make their pies. For this recipe, I like to use frozen puff pastry.

Preheat oven to 400°F. Thaw the pastry and fit one sheet into a 9-inch square baking pan. Cut the remaining pastry into 24 ½-inch strips.

In a large bowl, combine the raspberries, blueberries, cornstarch, and sugar. Turn into the pastry-lined pan. Place the pastry strips on top of the filling in a lattice pattern.

Bake for 20 to 25 minutes, or until the filling bubbles and the pastry is lightly browned. Serve hot or warm.

6 to 8 servings

1 package (16 ounces) frozen puff pastry, thawed

2 cups fresh raspberries, or frozen unsweetened raspberries

2 cups fresh blueberries, or frozen unsweetened blueberries

3 tablespoons cornstarch

⅓ cup sugar

Mustikka-vadelmapiirakka

FINNISH MAY DAY PASTRIES

SNACKS &

COFFEE TABLES

SNACKS IN THE FINNISH SAUNA

In Finland, an invitation to "sauna" is also an invitation to share food. In the summertime, in the countryside, the snack most often consumed is sausages and beer. Sometimes the sausages are wrapped in foil and cooked on the hot rocks of the sauna stove, or on a special grill in the fireplace in the dressing room. The sausages and beer are usually followed by coffee, breads, cakes, pastries, and cookies. ∎ The sauna is preheated to somewhere between 180°F and 200°F. Personally, I am not interested in anything under 180°F. Then it is into the dressing room to undress (it is customary for men and women to sauna separately in the nude, or for families to sauna together naked), grab a towel to sit on and maybe a cloth to breathe through

MENU

SAUNA-COOKED SAUSAGES

HOMEMADE DILL MUSTARD

CARAWAY RYE BUNS

DILL PICKLES

BEER, SOFT DRINKS, CHILLED JUICES

for moisture, and then head for the highest shelf in the sauna. There is a difference between a dry-heat sauna and a wet-heat or steam sauna. I prefer the dry heat, which gets much hotter. I sit and switch myself with birch twigs—they smell wonderful when dipped in water and set on the hot rocks of the sauna for a few seconds, and that also provides just the right amount of moisture in the air. Then, when hot enough, it is time to run outside and jump in the lake, or roll in the snow, or douse myself with a bucket of cold water to cool off. Afterwards, it's back to the sauna for more. That's the time to put a ring of sausage on top of the sauna stones, and when it's hot and sizzling, to retire to the dressing room for a snack of sausage and cold beer.

In Finland, there is a special sausage called "sauna sausage." The best substitute we have in the United States is a well-prepared ring bologna. Some people have an open fireplace in the dressing room of their sauna where they will grill the sausages—on the end of a stick or long fork. In the summertime, many Finns cook their sausages on a fire pit outside of the sauna. Of course, in place of sauna stones, you can cook the sausage on a barbecue grill, in a fireplace, or in the oven. To eat them, Finns usually spear the sausage with a fork and nibble on it, occasionally dipping it in mustard.

1 pound ring bologna

Wrap the bologna in foil, enclosing it with the seam of the foil on the side. Place it on the hot sauna stove rocks for 5 minutes. Turn over and cook for another 5 minutes, or until the bologna sizzles. Remove onto a platter and unwrap. Serve with mustard.

4 servings

Saunamakkara

HOMEMADE DILL MUSTARD

¼ cup mustard powder

⅓ cup sugar

2 tablespoons white wine vinegar

2 tablespoons heavy (whipping) cream

1 tablespoon chopped fresh dill, or 2
    teaspoons dried dill weed

It's a good idea to double this recipe so that you will have enough for awhile. Store the mustard in an airtight jar in the refrigerator.

In a small bowl, stir together the mustard powder, sugar, and vinegar, until the sugar is dissolved. Add the cream and mix well. Stir in the dill. Turn into a serving bowl and let stand for at least 30 minutes before serving.

Approximately ½ cup

Hjemmelavet sennep

Hjemmelaget sennep

Hemlagad senap

These buns go well with grilled sausages and homemade mustard.

In a large bowl, dissolve the yeast in the warm water. Add the molasses (or corn syrup) and let stand for 5 minutes, or until the yeast foams. Add the caraway seeds, salt, butter (or other fat), milk, and rye flour and beat well.

Stir in the bread (or unbleached all-purpose) flour, one cupful at a time, until the dough is stiff and will not absorb more flour. Cover and let rest for 15 minutes.

Turn the dough out onto a board sprinkled with flour, and knead, adding more flour as necessary, until the dough is smooth and satiny, about 10 minutes. Wash and grease the bowl, then place the dough in it and turn it over to grease the top. Cover and let rise until doubled, about 1 hour.

Cover with parchment paper or lightly grease two baking sheets.

Turn the dough out onto a lightly oiled board. Divide it into quarters, then divide the quarters into quarters again, to make sixteen equal-sized portions of dough. Shape each portion into a long, narrow bun and place on one of the prepared baking sheets. Let rise until puffy, 30 to 45 minutes.

Preheat oven to 400°F. Pierce each roll all over with a fork. Bake for 15 minutes, or until golden.

16 buns

CARAWAY RYE BUNS

2 packages active dry yeast

½ cup warm water (105°F to 115°F)

2 tablespoons light molasses or dark corn syrup

1 tablespoon caraway seeds

2 teaspoons salt

2 tablespoons butter or other fat, melted

2 cups skim milk, scalded and cooled to lukewarm

2 cups light or dark rye flour

4 to 4½ cups bread or unbleached all-purpose flour

Ruispullat

Rågbullar

CELEBRATION COFFEE TABLE

In Scandinavia, life's important occasions—a baby's baptism, an adolescent's confirmation, an engagement, an anniversary, a milestone birthday—are celebrated by family and friends with a special spread of cakes, cookies, and pastries laid out on a ceremonious coffee table. Every Scandinavian knows the ritual. With the first cup of coffee, you sample a sweet yeast bread and a couple of small cakes or a wide variety of butter cookies. With the second cup of coffee, you taste the unfrosted sponge or pound cake and more cookies. With the third cup of coffee, you enjoy a rich, fancy, cream-covered or frosted torte. Traditionally, the perfect coffee table has seven different items on it, following the basic pattern of this menu. In this day and age, however, it is perfectly acceptable to select just the cardamon-flavored sweet bread and a sampling of cookies when entertaining only a few guests. Coffee is still the preferred drink for this sort of celebration, although a few Scandinavians will choose to serve tea as well. In Scandinavia, a coffee table such as this one is easy to prepare for there are local bakeries everywhere whose high-quality baked goods taste just like homemade. If you are determined to make this menu from scratch but find it a bit daunting, keep in mind that all these treats can be made in advance and frozen.

MENU

SCANDINAVIAN COFFEE BRAID

CARDAMOM CREAM CAKE

ALMOND BUTTER TARTS

SWEDISH NUT TORTE

OLD-FASHIONED JELLY COOKIES

BROWNED BUTTER
COOKIE "DREAMS"

SPONGE CAKE

This sweet yeast dough flavored with cardamom is versatile. It can be shaped into braids, as in this recipe, or made into buns or rolls, or it can be rolled out and filled with ground nuts, marzipan, or fresh fruit jams. In addition, sometimes the dough is patted into a buttered square or round pan, topped with sugar and almonds, and frosted. For the holidays, Norwegians and Danes add candied fruits and nuts and shape the dough into round loaves. The Swedes use essentially the same recipe but substitute saffron for cardamom to make a festive Christmas bread.

I n a large bowl, dissolve the yeast in the warm water. Let stand for 5 minutes, until the yeast bubbles. Stir in the milk, sugar, salt, cardamom, eggs, and 4 cups of the flour. Beat until smooth. Add the butter.

Gradually stir in enough of the remaining flour to make a stiff dough. Turn out onto a floured board. Cover and let stand for 15 minutes. Wash and grease the bowl and set it aside.

Knead the dough, adding flour as necessary, until it is smooth, about 10 minutes. Place the dough in the prepared bowl, turning the dough to grease it on all sides. Cover and let rise in a warm place until doubled in bulk, 1½ to 2 hours. Punch down. Turn the dough out onto an oiled surface and divide it into three parts. Divide each part into three or four portions. Roll each portion into a 30-inch-long rope.

Braid three or four ropes together to make a loaf. Pinch the ends together and tuck them under the loaf. Place on a lightly greased baking sheet and repeat with the remaining portions of dough. Let rise in a warm place, until almost doubled, about 45 minutes.

Preheat oven to 375°F. Brush the loaves with the egg-milk mixture and sprinkle with the almonds and/or sugar. Bake for 25 to 30 minutes or until lightly browned. Do not overbake. Cool on racks.

3 loaves

2 packages active dry yeast

½ cup warm water (105°F to 115°F)

2 cups milk, scalded and cooled

1 cup sugar

2 teaspoons salt

1 teaspoon freshly crushed cardamom

4 eggs, slightly beaten

8 to 9 cups flour

½ cup (1 stick) butter, melted

1 egg beaten with 2 tablespoons milk

½ cup sliced almonds

½ cup pearl sugar or coarsely crushed sugar cubes

Hvedebrød
Pulla
Hvetebrød
Vetebröd

CARDAMOM CREAM CAKE

2 cups flour

1 cup sugar

2 teaspoons baking powder

1 teaspoon freshly ground cardamom

⅛ teaspoon salt

3 eggs, at room temperature

1½ cups heavy (whipping) cream

Powdered sugar

Pound cakes flavored with cardamom are popular in all of Scandinavia. Use only freshly ground cardamom as the kind that is sold pre-ground has little flavor.

Preheat oven to 350°F. Butter a 9-inch fancy or plain tube pan and dust with flour.

In the large bowl of an electric mixer, combine the flour, sugar, baking powder, cardamom, and salt. Blend in the eggs at low speed. Add the cream and beat at high speed, scraping the bowl, until the batter is the texture of softly whipped cream. Turn the batter into the prepared pan. Bake for 50 to 60 minutes or until the cake tests done (a wooden skewer inserted into the center of the cake will come out clean). Cool for 5 minutes in the pan. Invert onto a rack and cool completely. Dust with powdered sugar before serving.

8 to 10 servings

Kardemommekage

Kardemummakakku

Kardemommekake

Kardemummakaka

SCANDINAVIAN FEASTS

To make this recipe, you need special tartlet pans called "Sandbak-kelse Tart Forms." They are sold in an assortment of shapes and sizes in most Scandinavian gift stores and mail-order catalogs and usually come eighteen to a set. The tarts can be served plain or filled with jam or berries and whipped cream.

In a large bowl, cream the butter and sugar until well blended. Add the egg, almonds, and flour and mix well. Shape the dough into a roll about 2 inches thick.

Preheat oven to 325°F. Coat the insides of the tartlet pans with nonstick cooking spray and dust lightly with flour. Slice the chilled roll of dough into ¼-inch-thick pieces. Place each slice into a tartlet pan and, with flour-coated thumbs, press the dough evenly into the pans.

Place the filled pans on a baking sheet and bake for about 10 minutes, or until light brown. Cool. Tap the tins lighty to remove the tarts.

Approximately 40 2½-inch tart shells

ALMOND BUTTER TARTS

1 cup (2 sticks) butter, softened

½ cup sugar

1 egg, slightly beaten

½ cup ground or finely pulverized blanched almonds

2½ cups flour

SWEDISH NUT TORTE

½ cup (1 stick) butter

2¼ cups sugar

6 eggs, separated

⅓ cup flour

2 teaspoons baking powder

⅓ cup milk

1 cup chopped filberts or walnuts

FILLING

2 cups heavy (whipping) cream

2 tablespoons powdered sugar

Additional chopped nuts, for garnish

Fresh strawberries, for garnish
(optional)

This festive dessert is named after the town of Glomminge on the Swedish island of Oland. It is sometimes called "Mamma's Favorite Torte."

Line an 11-by-17-inch jelly-roll pan with parchment paper and butter the paper. Preheat oven to 350°F.

In a large bowl, cream the butter and 1 cup of the sugar until fluffy and light. Add the egg yolks and beat until very light in texture. Stir in the flour, baking powder, and milk. Spread the batter in the prepared pan. Sprinkle half of the nuts on top.

In a medium-sized bowl, beat the egg whites and the remaining sugar until stiff, to form a meringue. Spread the meringue over the batter. Top with the remaining nuts.

Bake for 25 minutes, or until a toothpick inserted in the center of the cake comes out clean. Remove from the pan, peel off the parchment paper, and cool. Cut the cake into two equal halves.

To prepare the filling, in a large bowl, whip the cream and sugar until stiff peaks form. Spread half of the whipped cream over one half of the torte, meringue-side up. Cover with the other half of the torte, meringue-side up. Before serving, top with the remaining whipped cream and the chopped nuts. Garnish with strawberries, if desired.

16 servings

Glomminge Torte

These buttery sandwich cookies are very delicate. When cutting them out, don't let the diameter exceed two inches.

2 cups flour

In a large mixing bowl or food processor, combine the flour, butter, ½ cup of the sugar, and the egg yolk and blend until a smooth dough is formed. Wrap with plastic wrap and chill for 30 minutes.

1 cup (2 sticks) butter, at room temperature, cut into slices

½ cup plus 2 to 3 tablespoons sugar

Preheat oven to 350°F. On a lightly floured board, roll the dough out to a ⅛-inch thickness. Cut out an even number of 2-inch rounds. Using a thimble or ½-inch round cookie cutter, cut the center out of half of the rounds. Brush the rounds with the centers cut out with egg white and sprinkle with the almonds and the remaining sugar. Leave the remaining rounds plain.

1 egg, separated

⅓ cup finely chopped almonds

Approximately ⅓ cup jam or jelly

Cover with parchment paper or lightly grease several baking sheets. Place the cookies on the prepared baking sheets and bake for 10 to 12 minutes, until set and just barely golden around the edges. Transfer the cookies to wire racks to cool.

Top the cookies without holes with about ½ teaspoon fruit jelly or jam. Place the cookies with holes over the jam, almond-sugar side up, to make sandwiches.

Approximately 50 cookies

Syltetøjskager

Hillokakut

Syltetøykaker

Syltkakor

BROWNED BUTTER COOKIE "DREAMS"

1 cup (2 sticks) unsalted butter

¾ cup sugar

1 egg yolk

2 teaspoons vanilla extract

½ teaspoon freshly ground cardamom

⅛ teaspoon salt

2 cups flour

1 egg white

⅓ cup blanched whole almonds

½ cup powdered sugar

These little cookies are so tender and light they virtually melt in your mouth. The dough is flavored with browned butter and with cardamom, a favorite baking spice throughout Scandinavia.

In a heavy skillet, over medium-low heat, without stirring, melt the butter and allow it to brown (it should take about 15 minutes). Strain the browned butter through a fine sieve into a metal mixing bowl. Place over a bowl of cold water and chill until firm. Stir in the sugar, egg yolk, vanilla, cardamom, and salt. Beat until light and fluffy.

Preheat oven to 350°F. Slowly blend in the flour, until the dough is well blended and smooth. Roll the dough into small balls, using about 2 measuring teaspoons of dough for each one.

Place the dough balls on ungreased baking sheets. Dip the almonds into the egg white, then press one into the center of each cookie. Bake for 12 to 15 minutes, until the cookies are set but not yet colored. Transfer to a wire rack and dust with powdered sugar.

Approximately 70 cookies

Drømme

Unelmat

Drømmer

Drömmar

This cake is also known as "Sunday Cake" because in many Scandinavian homes it is baked as a special weekend treat.

Preheat oven to 350°F. Butter a 9-inch tube pan and dust generously with the vanilla wafer crumbs. In a medium-sized bowl, stir together the flour and baking powder. In a large bowl, beat the eggs with the sugar, until light and fluffy. In a saucepan, heat the water to boiling and add the butter. Heat again until the butter is melted and the mixture comes to a boil.

Add the flour mixture and the water-butter mixture to the beaten eggs and whisk until smooth. Pour into the prepared cake pan. Bake for 1 hour or until the cake springs back when touched in the center. Cool the cake in the pan. Cut into slices to serve.

Approximately 12 servings

SPONGE CAKE

¼ to ½ cup vanilla wafer crumbs

1½ cups flour

2 teaspoons baking powder

3 eggs

1 cup sugar

½ cup water

¼ cup (½ stick) butter

1 tablespoon grated lemon rind

Sukkerbrødskage

Sokerikakku

Sukkerbrød

Sockerkaka

FINNISH MAY DAY PARTY

The first of May has come to be celebrated as the beginning of summer because it is when the daylight hours actually begin to exceed the hours of darkness. It is a legal holiday in Finland as well as in Sweden. In Helsinki, university students celebrate all day and night and compete to place their white university caps on the head of Amanda, the stone goddess on the waterfront. Street vendors clutching colorful clouds of helium-filled balloons attract small children on every corner. The air vibrates with music, and almost everybody has an open house, offering *tippaleipä* (a fried pastry) and *sima* (a homemade sparkling lemon drink). From that day until the end of the summer, *sima* is the preferred soft drink. *Sima* takes about five days to make, and with all the variety of fizzy drinks available commercially, you might wonder why bother? But making *sima* reminds me of summers when we used to make root beer, and both the drinks and the memories are well worth the trouble. ■ Although traditions vary, some call for herring and icy schnapps on the morning menu for May Day to ensure that the summer will be a good one. I have added Swedish hamburgers to this menu, but at Finnish May Day gatherings, *sima* and *tippaleipä* are the mainstays.

MENU

**HOMEMADE SPARKLING
LEMON DRINK**

FINNISH MAY DAY PASTRIES

PICKLED HERRING

ICED SCHNAPPS

**SWEDISH BEEF PATTIES WITH BEETS
AND CAPERS**

GREEN SALAD

FRESH STRAWBERRIES

It takes about five days to make *sima*. You will need at least five one-quart bottles with screw-on tops.

With a potato peeler, remove the zest (the yellow part of the rind) from the lemon and place it in a large nonaluminum pot. Slice the lemon and set aside. Add the water, brown sugar, and granulated sugar to the pot and bring it to a boil (this is to destroy any bacteria that could affect the flavor), stirring until the sugars dissolve. Remove the pot from the heat, cover, and cool to about 110°F. Stir in the sliced lemon and yeast. Cover and let stand at room temperature until the following day, when the *sima* should develop little bubbles around the edges. Strain the mixture through a fine sieve.

Sterilize five 1-quart jars with screw-on tops by filling them with water and boiling them in a pot of water for 20 minutes. Pour the strained *sima* into the sterilized jars. Add 1 teaspoon granulated sugar and 2 raisins to each jar. Seal the bottles and store them in a cool place until the raisins rise to the surface, about 2 to 4 days. Chill until ready to serve.

5 quarts

1 lemon

5 quarts water

½ cup brown sugar

½ cup granulated sugar

¼ teaspoon active dry or compressed yeast

Additional granulated sugar and raisins for each bottle

Sima

FINNISH MAY DAY PASTRIES

Oil for frying

3 eggs

¾ cup sugar

2 cups flour

¼ cup beer or sparkling mineral water

Powdered sugar

These pastries are simple to make—you drizzle the thin batter into hot fat to make a birds nest. In Finland, they are traditionally eaten on May Day, along with the sparkling lemon drink *sima*.

In a deep pot or fryer, heat the oil (approximately 3 inches deep) to 375°F.

In a large bowl, beat the eggs and sugar until thick and frothy. Blend in the flour and beer (or water) to make a smooth batter. Turn the batter into a heavy-duty sealable plastic bag and snip off one of the bottom corners.

Drizzle about ⅓ cup batter through the opening into the hot fat, swirling it into a coiled shape about 3 inches in diameter. Fry for 1 minute on each side or until golden brown. Use a slotted spoon to lift the cooked pastries from the oil. Drain on paper towels. Dust with powdered sugar. Serve hot.

15 pastries

Tippaleipä

Krumelurer

SWEDISH BEEF PATTIES WITH BEETS AND CAPERS

The tang of pickled beets gives these hamburgers a distinctive flavor.

In a large bowl, mix together the beef, beet liquid, bread crumbs, salt, and pepper, until well blended. Add the egg, beets, and capers. Shape into eight patties. In a heavy skillet, warm the butter, and add the patties. Cook the patties for 3 to 4 minutes on each side, until done to your liking. Serve with lingonberry preserves.

4 servings

1 pound extra-lean ground beef

½ cup liquid from pickled beets

¼ cup fine dry bread crumbs

1 teaspoon salt

¾ teaspoon freshly ground black pepper

1 egg

½ cup finely-chopped pickled beets

¼ cup capers, drained and chopped

Butter

Lingonberry preserves

Lindstrommin Pihvi

Biff a la Lindström

CHRISTMAS COFFEE TABLE

The most opulent coffee tables of Scandinavia are those of the Christmas season. There are always at least ten different kinds of cookies and five kinds of cake. In addition to the traditional fruit-stuffed bread and the butter and gingerbread cookies, the Norwegians include *krumkaker, avletter,* and *goro,* all of which are made one cookie at a time in irons on the stove. *Krumkaker* are rolled into cone or cigar shapes while they are still hot from the iron. *Avletter* are large, flat, scroll-embossed cookies, and *goro* are rectangular in shape and are stacked like crackers on a platter. The Finns tend to limit their cookie choices to a modest selection of butter cookies and gingersnaps cut into all of the traditional shapes—stars, hearts, boys, and girls—as well as the shape of a pig. The Finns and Swedes consider Christmas Stars, the prune-filled star-shaped pastries, the preeminent treat on the Christmastime coffee table. And don't forget, there is always plenty of good, strong coffee. ▪ Most Scandinavian cooks do their own baking for their holiday coffee tables. To manage this, everything is baked ahead of time and frozen, or kept in a cool, dry place, each individual item sealed in airtight tins or plastic bags or wrap. Cool, dry, and airtight are especially important so that crisp cookies stay crisp and cakes and breads stay moist and fresh. All of these items can be made up to three months in advance and frozen, or up to a month in advance and kept in a cool place.

MENU

FRUITED CHRISTMAS BREAD

ROSETTES

NORWEGIAN SWEET CRACKERS

NORWEGIAN CURLED COOKIES

RYE COOKIES

SPICY GINGER COOKIES

BASIC BUTTER COOKIES
AND VARIATIONS

NORWEGIAN ROLLED COOKIES

OLD-FASHIONED FLAT CAKES

CHRISTMAS STARS

CHRISTMAS CRULLERS

LINGONBERRY JAM CAKE

◎◎◎◎

Cardamom is optional here, as are the candied fruits, but in Norway and Denmark, it's not Christmas without this traditional fruited bread.

In a large mixing bowl, dissolve the yeast in the warm water and let stand for 5 minutes, or until the yeast foams. Beat in the milk, sugar, butter, eggs, salt, and cardamom (if using). Stir in half the flour and beat well. Add enough of the remaining flour to make a soft dough. Cover and let rest for 15 minutes.

Turn the dough out onto a lightly floured board. Knead for 10 minutes, or until the dough is smooth and satiny. Knead in the raisins and candied fruits (if using). Wash the bowl, lightly grease it, then return the dough to it. Turn the dough over so that it is greased on all sides. Cover and let rise in a warm place until doubled, 45 minutes to 1 hour. Punch down and let rise again until doubled in bulk, 45 minutes to 1 hour.

Butter three 8- or 9-inch round cake pans. Turn dough out onto a lightly oiled work surface. Divide the dough into three equal parts. Shape each portion into a smooth round loaf and place in a baking pan, smooth-side up. Cover and let rise until doubled, 45 minutes to 1 hour.

Preheat oven to 375°F. Stir together the egg and milk to make the egg wash. Brush the tops of the loaves with the egg wash and sprinkle with sugar and/or almonds. Bake for 25 to 30 minutes, until golden and a wooden skewer inserted in the center comes out clean. Cool loaves in their pans on wire racks.

To prepare the glaze, in a small bowl, stir together the powdered sugar, 2 tablespoons of the cream, and the almond extract, until smooth. Add the remaining tablespoon of cream, if necessary. Remove loaves from pans and spread an equal amount of glaze on each.

3 loaves

2 packages active dry yeast

½ cup warm water (105°F to 115°F)

2 cups milk, scalded and cooled to lukewarm

½ cup sugar

½ cup (1 stick) butter, softened

2 eggs, beaten

2 teaspoons salt

1 teaspoon freshly ground cardamom (optional)

7 to 8 cups flour

1 cup golden or dark raisins

1 cup mixed candied fruits (optional)

EGG WASH

1 egg

2 tablespoons milk

Pearl sugar, crushed sugar cubes, and/or chopped almonds

ALMOND GLAZE

1 cup powdered sugar

2 to 3 tablespoons heavy (whipping) cream

½ teaspoon almond extract

Julekage

Julekake

ROSETTES

1¼ cups water or light-colored beer

1 egg

1 cup flour

2 teaspoons sugar

Pinch of salt

Fat or oil for frying

Powdered sugar

These crisp cookies can be made into many fanciful shapes, including butterflies, snowflakes, and stars, depending on the shape of the iron. Rosette irons are sold in specialty cooking shops as well as in most large department stores.

In a bowl, whisk together the water (or beer), egg, flour, sugar, and salt, until smooth. Cover and refrigerate for at least 1 hour. Heat approximately 3 inches or more of fat (or oil) to 375°F. Place the rosette iron in the fat (or oil) to preheat. Lift the iron up and allow it to drip dry, then dip two thirds of the iron into the batter. Do not dip it further in or you will not be able to remove the rosette after frying. Hold the iron over the fat for 10 seconds, then lower it into the fat (or oil) and fry until the batter is golden brown, about 1 minute. Gently remove the rosette with the help of a fork and drain on paper toweling. Repeat with all of the batter.

Dust fried pastries with powdered sugar. Store in an air-tight tin in a cool, dry place, until ready to serve.

Approximately 36 rosettes

COOKIE CUTTERS AND TINS

ALMOND WREATH CAKE RINGS

ROSETTE IRONS

NORWEGIAN SWEET CRACKERS

3 eggs

1 cup sugar

1 cup heavy (whipping) cream,
    whipped

1 cup (2 sticks) butter, melted

¼ teaspoon salt

1 teaspoon freshly ground cardamom

1 teaspoon grated lemon peel

6 cups flour

Goro, like *krumkaker* and *avletter,* date back to the times when pastries were baked over an open fire. The *goro* iron is rectangular in shape and imprints a pattern of flowers and leaves on the crisp cracker-like pastries.

Cut a paper pattern the same size as the *goro* iron. Set aside. In a large bowl, combine all of the ingredients in the order given, mixing until thoroughly blended. The dough will be stiff. Divide the dough into four equal pieces. On a lightly floured surface, roll each piece into a ⅛- to ¹⁄₁₆-inch-thick rectangle. Cut the dough into the shape of the paper pattern. Place the *goro* iron on the stovetop and preheat it over medium heat, until a drop of water sizzles and bounces when dropped on the iron. Brush the inside of the iron with shortening. Place one piece of the dough on the hot iron. Close the iron and bake over medium heat for 1 to 2 minutes on each side, until golden brown. Remove the cracker from the iron. Cool on a rack. Repeat with the remaining dough. Separate into individual crackers.

Approximately 36 crackers

Goro

The round *krumkake* iron is beautifully decorated with swirls and curls. The cookies are pliable while they are hot and can be shaped around a wooden cone, or can be draped in a cup, and later filled with fruit and whipped cream.

In a medium bowl, combine the sugar, eggs, and butter. Whisk in the milk, until the mixture is smooth. Stir in the flour until blended. Add the cardamom. Preheat the *krumkake* iron over medium heat until a drop of water sizzles when dropped on top. Lightly brush the inside top and bottom of the iron with shortening, oil, or melted butter. Spoon 1 tablespoon of the batter onto the center of the hot iron. Close the iron and bake for about 1 minute on each side, or until the cookie is lightly browned. Insert the tip of a knife under the cookie to remove it from the iron. Roll the hot cookie into a cigar or cone shape. Cool on a rack. Cookies become crisp as they cool. Repeat with the remaining batter. If the batter becomes thick, stir in water, 1 tablespoon at a time.

25 to 30 cookies

1 cup sugar

2 eggs

½ cup (1 stick) butter, melted

⅔ cup milk

1⅓ cups flour

1 teaspoon crushed cardamom seeds

Water, if necessary

Krumkaker

CHRISTMAS COFFEE TABLE COOKIES

RYE COOKIES

1 cup (2 sticks) butter

½ cup sugar

1 cup light rye flour

1¼ cups all-purpose flour

2 tablespoons ice water

This delicate and buttery dough is rolled thin and cut into rounds with a little hole in the center to resemble in miniature the large loaves of rye bread that are eaten all year round.

In a large bowl, cream the butter with the sugar, until smooth. Add the rye flour, then the all-purpose flour, and mix until well blended. Blend in the ice water. Gather into a ball and chill for 30 minutes or until firm enough to handle.

Cover with parchment paper or lightly grease several baking sheets. Preheat oven to 350°F.

Divide the dough into quarters and knead lightly to make them pliable. On a lightly floured surface, roll out each portion to a ⅛-inch thickness. Cut into a 2½-inch round and pierce all over with a fork. With a small cookie cutter or bottle cap, cut a round hole in the center of each cookie.

Bake for 8 to 10 minutes, or until firm and beginning to brown on the edges. Cool on parchment paper, or on racks.

48 cookies

Ruiskakut

Rågkakor

Scholars believe that the tradition of making animal-shaped cookies, breads, and decorations during the holiday season dates back to pagan times when animals were slaughtered at harvest festivals to appease the gods. Poor people, who had no animals to offer, substituted animal-shaped breads.

These cookies are nice and spicy. The dough is simple to make and can be cut into all the traditional shapes, such as pigs, people, stars, and hearts.

In a large bowl, cream the butter and sugar until blended. Add the cinnamon, ginger, and cloves. In a separate bowl, combine the baking soda and boiling water, then add to the dough along with the flour. Mix to make a stiff dough. If necessary, add more water, one tablespoon at a time. Chill for 30 minutes.

Preheat oven to 375°F. Line several baking sheets with parchment paper. Roll the dough out to a ⅛-inch thickness. Cut into cookies using a 2-inch pig-shaped cookie cutter (or any other cookie cutter shape—such as a heart, star, boy, or girl—to make cookies that measure approximately 2 inches).

Place cookies on the prepared sheets and bake for 7 to 10 minutes, until lightly browned.

To prepare the icing, combine the egg white, powdered sugar, and almond extract. Turn into a pastry bag with a fine tip, or into a cone made of waxed paper with the bottom snipped off to form a fine tip, and decorate the cookies with names, scrolls, outlines, or any other patterns.

Approximately 60 cookies

SPICY GINGER COOKIES

⅔ cup (1 stick plus 2⅔ tablespoons) butter

¾ cup firmly packed brown sugar

1 tablespoon cinnamon

2 teaspoons ginger

1½ teaspoons ground cloves

1 teaspoon baking soda

¼ cup boiling water

2½ cups flour

ICING

1 egg white

3 cups powdered sugar

1 teaspoon almond extract

Brune kager

Nissu nassu

Brune kaker

Pepparkakor

BASIC BUTTER COOKIES

1 cup (2 sticks) butter, softened

½ cup sugar

1 egg yolk

2½ cups flour

Scandinavian homemakers often keep this basic cookie dough on hand to quickly bake into a variety of shapes. With just slight variations, it can made into butter fingers, spritz cookies, refrigerator cookies, or nut cookies.

Cream the butter with the sugar and egg yolk. Blend in the flour to make a smooth dough. Some of the variations below require further ingredients, some require chilling the dough at this stage. Refer below for further instructions.

Butter Fingers

Chill the dough for 30 minutes or until firm enough to handle.

Preheat oven to 350°F. Cover with parchment paper or lightly grease a baking sheet.

Divide the dough into six parts. Roll each part between the palms of your hands and shape into long strands that are about ½-inch thick. Place the strands close together and brush with egg white. Cut into 1½-inch strips and then roll each strip in a mixture of ¼ cup chopped almonds and 3 tablespoons sugar. Place on a lightly greased or parchment-covered baking sheet.

Bake the cookies for 15 minutes, or until golden.

60 fingers

Spritz Cookies

Preheat oven to 350°F. Put the unchilled cookie dough in a spritz press and press it into long strips or fancy shapes onto an unbuttered baking sheet. Bake for 10 minutes, or until golden.

60 cookies

Mørdejskager

Murotaikinakakut

Mørdeigskaker

Mordegskakor

Refrigerator Cookies

Add 2 teaspoons vanilla extract to the basic cookie dough. Shape the dough into 2 rolls about 1½-inches thick. Roll the dough in a mixture of 1 tablespoon sugar and 1 tablespoon cocoa. Wrap in plastic wrap. Chill for 30 minutes or until firm enough to handle.

Preheat oven to 350°F. Using a sharp knife cut the rolls into ⅛-inch-thick slices and place on an ungreased baking sheet. Bake for 6 to 8 minutes, until firm but not browned.

60 cookies

Nut Cookies

Chill the dough for 30 minutes or until firm enough to handle.

Preheat oven to 350°F. Shape the basic cookie dough into balls with a diameter of about ¾-inch. Roll the balls in egg white, then in finely chopped filberts. Place on an ungreased baking sheet. Indent the center of each ball with your thumb.

Bake for 10 minutes, or until lightly browned. While the cookies are baking, melt 1 tablespoon butter with 1 ounce baking chocolate. Stir in ½ cup powdered sugar. When the cookies come out of the oven, transfer them to a rack. While still warm, dot the center of each one with the icing.

60 cookies

NORWEGIAN ROLLED COOKIES

¾ cup sour cream or heavy (whipping) cream

3 tablespoons cold water

¼ cup sugar

10 tablespoons flour

Called *strull* in Norwegian, these cookies are made in a *krumkake* iron, and then rolled into a very thin, tight roll by wrapping them around the handle of a wooden spoon.

In a medium-sized bowl, using a hand mixer, beat the cream, water, and sugar, until the batter is light and fluffy and looks like softly whipped cream. Measure the flour into a fine sieve and dust it over the top of the cream mixture. Using a rubber spatula, gently fold in the flour. Preheat the *krumkake* iron over medium heat until a drop of water sizzles when dropped on top. Lightly brush the inside top and bottom of the iron with shortening, oil, or melted butter. Spoon a heaping teaspoonful of the mixture into the preheated *krumkake* iron. Bake until pale golden, about one minute on each side. Remove the cookie from the iron and while still warm and flexible, roll it around the handle of a wooden spoon, then slide it off. The rolled cookie should be 1 to 1½ inches in diameter. Repeat with remaining batter. The cookies become firm very quickly as they cool.

Approximately 2 dozen cookies

OLD-FASHIONED FLAT CAKES

2 cups heavy (whipping) cream

1 cup sour cream

1⅓ to 1½ cups water

¼ teaspoon salt

2 teaspoons sugar

2¾ cups flour

These cookies, *Avletter* in their homeland, are the oldest known cookies in Norway. They are baked in either an *avlette* or *krumkake* iron.

In a large bowl, combine all of the ingredients and beat until the batter is smooth and the consistency of thick pancake batter. Preheat the *avlette* or *krumkake* iron over medium heat until a drop of water sizzles when dropped on top. Lightly brush the inside top and bottom of the iron with shortening, oil, or melted butter. One tablespoon at a time, spoon the batter onto the center of the heated iron. Close the iron and bake for 1 to 1½ minutes, just until pale golden. Remove from the iron and cool flat. Stack them to serve or to store.

60 flat cakes

CHRISTMAS STARS

Every Scandinavian cook has a favorite recipe for this classic Christmas pastry. I've provided directions for a quick cheese puff pastry, but feel free to substitute a 16-ounce package of the store-bought frozen variety.

To prepare the filling, place the prunes in a saucepan. Add the water and sugar and simmer for 20 minutes, or until the prunes are tender. Cool and purée.

Preheat oven to 450°F.

To prepare the pastry, measure the flour into a food processor fitted with a steel blade. Slice the butter into the flour. Process, using on/off pulses, until the butter is cut into pea-sized pieces. Add the cottage cheese and process until the pastry comes together in a ball (add 1 to 2 tablespoons ice water, if necessary).

Or, if using store-bought frozen puff pastry, thaw it out.

Roll out the pastry to make a 12-by-12-inch square. Cut the pastry into 3-inch squares, and place a level teaspoon of the prune mixture into the center of each one. Cut a 1½-inch slit from each corner toward the center. Fold alternate points into the center and press them together in the middle. Let rest on an ungreased baking sheet for 15 minutes. Brush with the beaten egg.

Bake for 10 minutes or until high, flaky, and golden.

16 pastries

PRUNE FILLING

1 (12-ounce) package pitted prunes

2 cups water

¼ cup sugar

PUFF PASTRY

2½ cups flour

1 cup (2 sticks) cold butter

1 cup creamed small-curd cottage cheese

1 to 2 tablespoons ice water, if necessary

CHRISTMAS CRULLERS

2 eggs

2 tablespoons heavy (whipping) cream

1 teaspoon vanilla extract

3 tablespoons sugar

1½ cups flour

Fat or oil for deep frying

Powdered sugar

The Norwegian name for these delicate, crisp, diamond-shaped cookies is *fattigman,* which translates to "poor man." They were named for the country cooks who originated the recipe.

In a large bowl, beat together the eggs, cream, and vanilla. Add the sugar and flour to make a stiff dough. On a lightly floured board, roll out the dough to a ⅛-inch thickness. Cut into 1-inch strips, then cut the strips diagonally, into 2½-inch-long pieces. Make a diagonal 1-inch-long slit between the two corners that are farthest apart. Pull one end of the dough through the slit to make a half-knot.

Heat the fat (or oil) to 375°F. Carefully lower the twisted dough into the hot fat (or oil). Cook for about 2 minutes, until golden brown on both sides. Drain on paper towels. Dust the cooled cookies with powdered sugar.

Approximately 60 cookies

Klejner

Klenetit

Fattigmän

Klenater

LINGONBERRY JAM CAKE

If you cannot find the lingonberry preserves called for in this recipe, substitute whole berry cranberry sauce or strained (to get rid of the seeds) raspberry jam. Moist and spicy, this cake can be made ahead of time, wrapped, and frozen. It actually slices more easily the day after it is baked.

Preheat oven to 350°F. Grease and flour a 9-by-5-inch loaf pan. In a large mixing bowl, cream the butter with the sugar and eggs, until light and fluffy. In a separate bowl, thoroughly mix the flour, cardamom, cinnamon, ginger, baking powder, baking soda, and salt. In another bowl, combine the sour cream and jam. Blend the dry ingredients and the sour cream mixture into the butter mixture, mixing until smooth. Turn into the prepared pan and bake for 55 to 60 minutes, or until a wooden skewer inserted in the center comes out clean. Let cool in the pan for 5 minutes, then turn out onto a rack to finish cooling.

One loaf

½ cup (1 stick) unsalted butter, at
    room temperature

1 cup sugar

2 eggs

1½ cups flour

1 teaspoon freshly ground cardamom

½ teaspoon ground cinnamon

½ teaspoon ground ginger

1 teaspoon baking powder

¼ teaspoon baking soda

¼ teaspoon salt

½ cup sour cream

½ cup lingonberry jam

| Lingonkage |
| Puolukkakakku |
| Lingonkake |
| Lingonkaka |

Adelost: A Swedish blue cheese made from cow's milk.

Aebelskivepande: A special pancake pan with rounded indentations designed to make *aebelskiver,* Danish pancakes.

Aebelskiver: Danish pancakes shaped like a round ball, called *munk* in Sweden and Norway and *munkki* in Finland.

Anchovies, Scandinavian: Sprats, small Baltic herrings, which are marinated in a sweet-salt brine, available in jars or tins, whole or fillets.

Aquavit: Translates literally to "water of life." A clear, herb- or seed-flavored spirit. The best known variety is caraway-flavored.

Avlette iron: A hinged iron used for making a Norwegian crisp cookie.

Avletter: A thin, crisp, flat Norwegian cookie made with a thin batter spooned into a heated *avlette* iron and cooked on both sides over range heat. *Avletter* are said to be the oldest known cookies in Norway.

Blini: A buckwheat crêpe, traditionally served on Shrove Tuesday in Finland. It is accompanied by *smetana* (a rich sour cream) and fresh burbot caviar.

Bondost: A soft, white, mild Swedish cow's-milk cheese.

Burbot: A freshwater codfish.

Cardamom: A member of the ginger family, this aromatic spice, which is native to India, is widely used in Scandinavia to flavor breads, cakes, and cookies. Because the essential oils of cardamom are easily lost as soon as the seeds are ground, it is best to grind the seed just before using. Purchase cardamom in its white, papery pod, remove the seeds from the pod and crush in a mortar with a pestle or in a coffee grinder.

Chard: Sometimes called Swiss Chard, it has dark green leaves with a reddish stalk. Available fresh in the summertime, and cooked in the same way as spinach.

Chokecherry: The edible berries of an ornamental shrub which is found wild in North America as well as in Scandinavia. These small cherries are very astringent and make excellent jams and jellies.

Cloudberry: Found in northern climes, a berry which looks like an amber-colored raspberry and has an aromatic flavor, which is not tart. Other names for the cloudberry are bake-apple berry, yellow berry, and mountain berry.

Coffee tables: A "coffee table" is a style of entertaining common throughout Scandinavia. The menu always includes coffee as the beverage and a variety of baked goods. The simplest coffee table usually includes a sweet yeast-raised bread, usually cardamom flavored. A complete coffee table includes a sweet yeast-raised bread, a poundcake without icing, and a fancy, filled cake, plus small cakes or cookies to number seven items in all. When partaking in a coffee table, one starts by sampling the bread, then the pound cake, then the fancy, filled cake, including the small cakes or cookies with each of the three "courses."

Crispbread: Bread dough that is rolled as thin as paper and baked on a griddle or in the oven until it is crisp.

Cured meat and fish: Meat and fish that has been air dried to preserve it. It may be treated with a salt or lime solution before drying. Cured meat and fish may be cold smoked. Fish may be soaked in flavored brines to preserve and flavor them.

Danablu: A Danish cow's-milk blue cheese.

Flatbread: A bread that may be a thin crispbread, or it may be a thin and flexible bread which is not crisp.

Fruit soup: A souplike preparation which is common to all Scandinavian countries, generally—but not always—served as a dessert.

Getost: Swedish goat's-milk cheese similar to Greek Feta cheese.

Gjetost: A faintly sweet, firm, caramel-colored, bricklike cheese, made from the whey of both cow's milk and goat's milk. This Norwegian cheese has a firm texture and is made by slowly cooking the whey until its sugars caramelize. This cheese is especially good thinly shaved and eaten on dark bread.

Glogg: A term used in Scandinavia for a hot punch. The usual connotation is that of a very alcoholic hot drink served during the winter holidays, but there are several nonalcoholic gloggs, too.

Gooseberries: Tart green berries which can be smooth or fuzzy. Rare in the United States, they flourish in northern Europe.

Goro: A crisp Norwegian cookie, baked in a special rectangular, hinged iron which is engraved with fancy scrolls.

Goro iron: A hinged iron which is heated on top of the stove. Used to cook *goro*, a special crisp Norwegian cookie. The iron measures about 4½ × 6½ inches and makes three rectangular cookies which you break apart after baking.

Graham flour: Whole wheat flour that is slightly coarser than regular grind.

Gravlax: A Scandinavian specialty of raw salmon cured in a salt-and-sugar mixture. After curing, it is sliced paper thin for serving.

Hardtack: A large, but thin, hard bread made with an unsalted, unleavened flour-and-water dough. After baking it is dried so that the bread can be stored for a long time.

Hardtack rolling pin: A rolling pin with hobnails used to roll out the hardtack dough, leaving a hobnail texture on top of the bread.

Havarti: A semisoft, mild, but slightly tangy, white Danish cheese named after the Danish experimental farm where it was developed.

Herring: A silvery saltwater fish, ranging from ¼ to 1 pound, popular in Scandinavia. Herring is often cured by salting, pickling, or smoking, but is also eaten fresh. There are over a hundred varieties of herring and they are found in cold waters of the north Atlantic and Pacific oceans.

Jarlsberg: A mild, creamy-colored, Norwegian cheese made in the Swiss style, with large irregular holes. It has a buttery texture and a sweet, nutty flavor.

Karelian rolling pin: A slim wooden rolling pin that is thicker in the center than at the edges.

Kransekake: Literally translates to "ring cake." A specialty of Norway, Denmark *(kransekage)* and Sweden *(kransekaka)*. The cake is made of graduated rings of baked dough, stacked into a pyramid shape. The traditional cake dough is made with almond paste, powdered sugar, and egg white.

Kringle: Designates a pretzel shape. Many breads and pastries are made in a pretzel shape and would be referred to as *kringles*.

Krumkaker: A Norwegian specialty. A fragile cookie that is baked in a special hinged iron on top of the stove. The cookie is flexible while hot and can be turned into a cone or roll, which stiffens and sets as it cools.

Krumkake iron: The special hinged iron in which *krumkaker* are baked. Today it is possible to buy electric irons which operate on the same principle as a waffle iron.

Lefse: One of a variety of Norwegian flatbreads. Lefse is generally a soft bread that can be folded or rolled. Many lefse recipes include potato as an ingredient. Crisp, dry varieties of lefse are moistened before serving so that they can be folded or rolled. Lefse is rolled thin and baked on a griddle or dry stove top.

Lefse rolling pin: A special grooved rolling pin. The grooves in the pin help the baker to roll dough out to paper-thinness. The grooves also leave a pattern on the bread.

Lingonberry: Called "cowberry" in other parts of the world. Lingonberry is a member of the cranberry family and grows wild in mountainous regions of Scandinavia. Lingonberries are available mostly as a preserve, and make an excellent accompaniment to potato pancakes and meats as well as desserts.

Lutefisk: A codfish which has been treated with lye before drying. The preparation of *lutefisk* is an ancient one, dating back into the early history of the Scandinavian countries, before salt was widely available. Although it is not necessarily a holiday treat in the Scandinavian countries, it has come to be known as a special holiday dish for Scandinavian-Americans.

Mace: Mace comes from the bright red membrane that covers the nutmeg seed. After it is removed and dried it becomes yellow-orange in color. Mace tastes and smells like a more pungent version of nutmeg. It is used in savory as well as sweet preparations.

Marzipan: A sweet mixture of almond paste, sugar, and unbeaten egg whites.

Mehu-maija: A three-tiered steam-process juicer from Finland. This unit is used to extract juices from all kinds of berries and fruits which are usually bottled or canned and used later as beverages and in sauces.

Mushrooms: A fleshy fungus, of which there are hundreds of varieties both cultivated and wild. Scandinavians, especially Finns, are avid hunters of wild mushrooms. They are dried, brined, or frozen and used in soups, sauces, pastries, and all sorts of dishes.

Nettle: A wild spring green, popular in Scandinavia when its leaves are tender and young, in the springtime. Nettles are used to flavor homemade cheese and soups.

Nökkelost: Also called *kuminost*. A Danish cheese made from whole or skimmed cow's milk. It is pale yellow and semifirm, flavored with cumin, caraway seed, and clove.

Pasha mold: A specially carved wooden mold used to press a special Easter dessert made with fresh cheese.

Pearl sugar: Sugar that resembles coarsely crushed sugar cubes. Used to garnish a variety of baked goods from cookies to sweet breads.

Platter or Plette pan: A specially indented cast-iron pan, used to make Swedish pancakes about 3 inches in diameter.

Potato Starch: A gluten-free flour made from cooked, dried, and ground potatoes. It is usually used as a thickener, but sometimes is used in cakes and cookies.

Potatoes: A tuber that originated in South America which is a staple in all of Scandinavia today.

Rahka: A fresh-milk cheese in Finland. Similar in texture and flavor to Italian ricotta.

Reindeer: A large game animal indigenous to Arctic regions. The meat tastes much the same as venison.

Remoulade: A classic French sauce, popular in Scandinavia, made by combining mayonnaise with mustard, capers, chopped gherkins, herbs, and anchovies. It is served chilled as an accompaniment to meat, fish, and shellfish as well as on open-faced sandwiches.

Rømmegrøt: Literally translates to "sour cream pudding." *Rømmegrøt* is a celebration food in Norway. Cooks carry their *rømmegrøt* to special events in elaborately decorated, covered wooden carriers. The design and the decoration of the carrier is often original and marks the cook with distinction.

Rosette: A deep-fried thin cruller, mostly associated with Swedish Christmas baking. Specially shaped irons are dipped into a thin batter, then into hot fat to cook the pastry.

Rusks: Twice-baked breads, which may be sweet or savory.

Saffron threads: The yellow-orange stigma of a special, small purple crocus. Each flower provides only three stigma, and they must be harvested by hand, then dried. It takes over 14,000 of these tiny stigmas to make one ounce of saffron. While saffron is used mainly in savory main dishes in Spain, it is most commonly used in baked goods in Scandinavia. Saffron-flavored sweet bread is a popular specialty of Sweden.

Sagablu: A rich blue-veined cheese produced in Denmark.

Salmon: A pink- to red-fleshed fish important to the cuisines of all of the Scandinavian countries. The most famous dish of Scandinavia, *gravlax*, is made of salmon. *Lax, lox,* and *lohi* are all Scandinavian words which mean "salmon."

Sandbakkelse tart forms: Little fancy tins which usually come in sets, used for making buttery tart shells. *Sandbakkelse* tart forms come in a variety of sizes ranging from 1 inch to about 2½ inches in diameter.

Scandinavian cheese shaver: A blunt spade-shaped utensil with an open blade cut across the wide part of the spade. Used to cut, or shave, thin slices of semihard or hard cheeses.

Smørrebrød: *Smørrebrød* designates open-faced sandwiches, most commonly attached to Danish cuisine.

Smorgasbord: This is a buffet style of service. The name literally translates to "bread-and-butter table." An authentic smorgasbord, however, has several varieties of breads, cheeses, cold fish and meats, and salads, considered to be the first course, followed by a variety of hot foods and desserts.

Spritz press: A metal device into which a pliable, buttery dough is placed. The dough is pressed through to make fancy shapes. Different shapes of spritz are made by changing the template or the tip of the spritz press.

Swedish brown beans: A variety of dried beans which look like a lighter version of common red beans. Available in Scandinavian specialty shops. Brown beans are cooked in the same manner as any dried bean, often flavored with a bit of ginger. Pinto beans or red beans are adequate substitutes for the Swedish brown bean.

Swedish yellow peas: Whole dried peas used for making Thursday Pea Soup. Slightly larger than whole dried peas commonly available, which can be used as a substitute for the Swedish yellow pea.

INDEX

CONVERSIONS

LIQUID MEASURES

FLUID OUNCES	U.S. MEASURES	IMPERIAL MEASURES	MILLILITERS
	1 TSP	1 TSP	5
¼	2 TSP	1 DESSERT SPOON	7
½	1 TBS	1 TBS	15
1	2 TBS	2 TBS	28
2	¼ CUP	4 TBS	56
4	½ CUP OR ¼ PINT		110
5		¼ PINT OR 1 GILL	140
6	¾ CUP		170
8	1 CUP OR ½ PINT		225
9			250, ¼ LITER
10	1¼ CUPS	½ PINT	280
12	1½ CUPS OR ¼ PINT		240
15		¾ PINT	420
16	2 CUPS OR 1 PINT		450
18	2¼ CUPS		500, ½ LITER
20	2½ CUPS	1 PINT	560
24	3 CUPS OR 1½ PINTS		675
25		1¼ PINTS	700
27	3½ CUPS		750
30	3¾ CUPS	1½ PINTS	840
32	4 CUPS OR 2 PINTS OR 1 QUART		900
35		1¾ PINTS	980
36	4½ CUPS		1000, 1 LITER

SOLID MEASURES

U.S. AND IMPERIAL MEASURES		METRIC MEASURES	
OUNCES	POUNDS	GRAMS	KILOS
1		28	
2		56	
3½		100	
4	¼	112	
5		140	
6		168	
8	½	225	
9		250	¼
12	¾	340	
16	1	450	
18		500	½
20	1¼	560	
24	1½	675	
27		750	¾
28	1¾	780	
32	2	900	
36	2¼	1000	1
40	2½	1100	
48	3	1350	
54		1500	1½

OVEN TEMPERATURE EQUIVALENTS

FAHRENHEIT	GAS MARK	CELSIUS	HEAT OF OVEN
225	¼	107	VERY COOL
250	½	121	VERY COOL
275	1	135	COOL
300	2	148	COOL
325	3	163	MODERATE
350	4	177	MODERATE
375	5	190	FAIRLY HOT
400	6	204	FAIRLY HOT
425	7	218	HOT
450	8	232	VERY HOT
475	9	246	VERY HOT

Design by Lynn Pieroni

The text of this book was set in Martin Gothic by
Graphic Arts Composition, Philadelphia, Pennsylvania.

This book was printed and bound by
Toppan Printing Company, Ltd., Tokyo, Japan.